Kevin's Kitchen

100 RECIPES
FOR DELICIOUS LIVING

BY
KEVIN LEE JACOBS

ISBN: 978-1-54390-842-8

Contents

Introduction

Shall we spend some time together, just the two of us? Good. I'd like to treat you to some of the most delicious foods on earth. We can start our day with crisp orange juice waffles topped with sweet, roasted strawberries. These we can wash down with cold-brewed coffee, because honestly, it's the best coffee of all. Then we can take a leisurely stroll through the gardens here, in search of pesto ingredients to accompany our afternoon cocktail. I hope you'll stay for dinner, too, because I'm planning Red Bell Pepper Soup for our first course, and Thyme and Wine Beef Stew for the main course. Just make sure to leave room for dessert, okay? It's a blueberry galette, sprinkled with crunchy Demerara sugar. I'll even show you how to make the galette's buttery crust. It's the same crust that French pastry chefs use, and all it requires is a food processor and about 30 seconds of your time.

What's that you say?

You'd like to know something about the kitchen and the house?

Well, it's an ordinary kitchen in a large Victorian that was built in 1826. The house was about 10 minutes from collapse when my husband, Will (a/k/a the "Silver Fox"), and I discovered it during a weekend get-away from our apartment in New York City. We purchased the place in 2002, and in time we not only saved the structure, but we restored it to its original 19th-century glory.

Behind our home is a series of gardens. These I created from scratch, and on a shoe-string budget, too. The formal boxwood garden was grown from cuttings. The raised beds in the herb and kitchen gardens are framed with inexpensive pine boards and rough-hewn hemlock. You see, I'm not a member of the proverbial "1-percent." I'm just 99-percent creativity!

While my two edible gardens are prolific, they are not large enough to provide all of the ingredients I need. Consequently I regularly shop for organic fruits, vegetables, and humanely-raised chicken and beef at local farm stands and farmers' markets. From time to time, I even visit the grocery store.

This book grew out of the recipes I developed for what has become a shockingly-popular website: A Garden for the House (www.agarden-forthehouse.com). I've added many more recipes that have not appeared on the site, and organized them as a series of occasions for you, your friends, and your family to enjoy:

Breakfast and Brunch — Hosting a Sunday Brunch? Prepare one of my make-ahead brunch casseroles on Saturday night. The next morning, you'll need only to turn on the oven before your guests arrive. Also included in this chapter: healthy granolas, sinful (and not-so-sinful) pancakes, colorful smoothies, and, and, and...

Small Savories and Sweets for Afternoon Tea or Anytime Snacks — Wanna live like a British aristocrat even when you're not? Then you must host a classy Afternoon Tea. You might be surprised to learn that traditional cream scones, small savory sandwiches, and attractive sweets can be prepared well in advance. I'll even show you how to make your own clotted cream!

Make-Ahead Cocktail Appetizers — Be a guest at your own cocktail party! Just gather some fresh, fragrant herbs from the garden (or farmers' market), and turn them into irresistible dips and spreads. Then whip up my easy, elegant, make-ahead canapés, and pour yourself a drink.

First Course Soups — I think a perfumed purée of a seasonal vegetable from the garden is the best (and also the easiest) way to start a dinner party. For cold-weather dining, I rely on butternut squash, garlic, and leeks. Warm weather invites lettuce and lovage, or a soup made from red bell peppers which is much more than the sum of its few ingredients.

Main Courses — You'll find these are suitable for either lunch or dinner. Because food-allergies and food-phobias are prevalent these days, I've included a number of mains that will satisfy both vegetarians and the gluten-intolerant. Almost all the recipes can be served year-round. But there is only one season in which to make the Tomato Pie on page 108, and that is late summer, when sun-ripened "love apples" can be plucked directly from the vine.

Delectable Desserts — I love sweets and hope you do, too. And there is a sweet treat for every season – berries in summer, apples in autumn, and lemons and chocolate for the rest of the year. You do like chocolate, yes?

CHAPTER ONE

Breakfast and Brunch

Cold-Brewed Coffee

How can we begin our day without coffee? Make mine cold-brewed, please.

Actually, cold-brewed coffee isn't "brewed" at all, since the method doesn't use hot water. The freshly-ground coffee beans are simply mixed with cold water, and then allowed to steep for 12-16 hours. As it steeps, the coffee acquires a remarkable chocolate aroma. It also develops an extremely smooth taste, without the slightest hint of bitterness. From reports I've read, cold-water steeping reduces acidity in coffee by up to 70%. And that's a good thing!

Ingredients for about 1 quart of coffee

1 cup coarsely-ground coffee beans

4 1/2 cups plain water

1) Pour the ground coffee into a bowl, a beaker, or an 8-cup glass measure. Add the water, and stir thoroughly to moisten the grinds. Cover with plastic wrap, and let steep for 12-16 hours. Steeping can occur either on the counter top or the refrigerator.

2) Set a fine mesh sieve over another bowl or beaker. Line the sieve with a piece of washed cheesecloth (or, just use paper towels). Strain the coffee through the sieve.

Cold-brewed coffee can be heated in the microwave without compromising the taste. For iced coffee, just add ice cubes!

Winter Squash Pancakes with Apple Cider Syrup

On a cold November morning, nothing makes my spirit soar like beta carotene-rich Winter Squash Pancakes. I like to top them with butter and Apple Cider Syrup, but they are equally delicious when dusted with confectioners' sugar, or drizzled with pure maple syrup.

Which winter squash to use? The decision is entirely yours. The pancakes pictured were made with butternut squash, sourced from my own garden. But I've also made pancakes with acorn squash from the farmers' market and canned pumpkin from the supermarket.

Ingredients for a dozen 3-inch pancakes

2 large eggs

3/4 cup winter squash, roasted and puréed

2 tablespoons pure maple syrup, plus additional for serving

4 tablespoons unsalted butter, melted

1 teaspoon cinnamon

a generous 1/4 teaspoon nutmeg

1 1/2 cups milk

2 cups all-purpose flour*

1 tablespoon baking powder*

a big pinch of kosher salt*

*If using self-rising flour, omit baking powder and salt

1) In a large bowl, whisk together the eggs, squash, maple syrup, butter, spices, and milk. In a separate, medium-size bowl, whisk to combine the flour, baking powder, and salt. Gradually add the dry ingredients to the wet, while stirring with a spoon or a spatula. Don't overmix — the batter should be somewhat lumpy.

2) Heat a skillet or griddle, and then spray it with non-stick spray. (I heat my electric skillet to 325°F.) The pan is ready when a drop of water dances on the surface.

3) Ladle, by the quarter cupful, the batter onto the hot surface. When air bubbles appear on top of the pancakes, flip them over and brown the other side.

If you are not going to serve the cakes right away, keep them warm in a 200°F oven. Serve, if you wish, with the following Apple Cider Syrup.

Apple Cider Syrup

Ingredients for about 2 cups of syrup

3/4 cup dark brown sugar

2 tablespoons cornstarch

1/2 teaspoon cinnamon

2 cups apple cider

3 tablespoons butter, cut into 3 pieces

In a heavy saucepan, whisk together the sugar, cornstarch, and cinnamon. Add the cider, and whisk to combine. While stirring occasionally, cook the mixture over medium heat until it boils and thickens. Add the butter, and stir constantly until the butter melts. Remove from heat. Serve warm over pancakes or waffles. You'll find the syrup is delicious on ice cream, too!

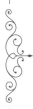

Cottage Cheese Pancakes

Would you believe these pancakes are low in carbohydrates? 'Tis true. I make them with lots of eggs and cottage cheese, but I use only a scant amount of flour. The eggs and cheese provide a light creaminess that everybody loves.

Ingredients for about 20 4-inch-diameter pancakes

6 large eggs

1 1/2 cups cottage cheese (any fat content you like)

1/2 teaspoon kosher salt

1/4 teaspoon baking powder

1/2 cup all-purpose flour

Optional Ingredients:
2 teaspoons sugar;
1/2 teaspoon
pure vanilla extract

1) Grease and preheat a skillet or griddle over a medium flame, or heat an electric skillet to 350°F. Put all ingredients into the jar of an electric blender. Blend at high speed until smooth – about 15 seconds.

2) Ladle, by the quarter cupful, the batter onto the hot skillet or griddle. When air bubbles appear along the edge of the pancakes, flip the cakes over to brown the other side.

Serve hot with butter, maple syrup, or any sweet substance that makes your tail wag.

Buckwheat Pancakes with Wild Blueberry Sauce

Buckwheat, if you've not yet made its acquaintance, is a "super food." It's rich in fiber, protein, and B vitamins. It's gluten-free, too. The nutty-tasting flour is simply the ground up seeds of the buckwheat plant, which goes by the unfortunate botanical name *Fagopyrum esculentum*. Use the flour for pancakes, and you won't be sorry. I like to top the cakes with Wild Blueberry Sauce.

Ingredients for 8
4-inch-diameter pancakes

1 cup buckwheat flour

1 tablespoon sugar

1 teaspoon baking powder

1 teaspoon baking soda

1/4 teaspoon kosher salt

1 1/4 cups buttermilk,
well-shaken

1 large egg

1 teaspoon pure vanilla extract

1) Grease and preheat a skillet or griddle over a medium flame. If using an electric skillet, preheat to 325°F. In a medium-size bowl, whisk together the flour, sugar, baking powder, baking soda, and salt. In a separate bowl (or a 4-cup glass measure), whisk together the buttermilk, egg, and vanilla extract. Add the wet ingredients to the dry, and whisk or stir just to combine. The mixture will be thick and bubbly.

2) Ladle the batter by the quarter cupful onto the hot skillet or griddle. When the cakes look dry around the edge, flip them over to brown the other side. Serve hot or warm with Wild Blueberry Sauce (or whatever topping floats your boat).

Wild Blueberry Sauce

Ingredients for about 2 cups of sauce

2 cups fresh or frozen wild blueberries

1/2 cup local honey

1 cup water

The juice of half a lemon (about 2 tablespoons)

2 tablespoons cornstarch, blended with 2 tablespoons water

In a medium saucepan, combine the blueberries, honey, water, and lemon juice. While stirring occasionally, bring the mixture to a low boil over medium heat. Add the cornstarch mixture, and stir just until the sauce thickens – about 1 minute. Serve warm over pancakes. Cooled, leftover sauce will be delicious on anything and everything.

Garbanzo Bean Pancakes

These pancakes are as soft and fluffy as ordinary wheat pancakes, but they are grain-free, gluten-free, and – because of their high fiber content – guilt-free. I think you'll love them.

Ingredients for about
8 4-inch-diameter
pancakes

1 cup garbanzo bean
(or "chick pea") flour

1 teaspoon baking powder

1/4 teaspoon kosher salt

1 cup milk

1 large egg

1 tablespoon olive oil

1 teaspoon pure
vanilla extract

1) In a large bowl, whisk together the flour, baking powder, and salt. In a medium bowl, whisk together the milk, egg, olive oil, and vanilla. Add the wet ingredients to the dry, and beat them with the wire whisk just to combine. Don't overmix –the batter should be somewhat lumpy.

2) Heat a skillet or griddle over a medium flame, or warm an electric skillet to 350°F. Lightly coat the skillet with vegetable spray.

3) Ladle, by the scant quarter-cupful, the batter onto the hot surface. When air bubbles appear along the edge of the pancakes, flip them over to brown the other side.

Serve hot, along with butter and local honey or warmed maple syrup.

Cranberry-Almond Granola

I make a batch of this crunchy, chewy, not-too-sweet cereal almost every week. It's delicious with yogurt for breakfast or brunch. It's also terrific for snacking (I sometimes shovel handfuls into my mouth when no one is watching), and for sprinkling over ice cream or poached fruit for dessert. For maximum crunch, be sure to use "old-fashioned" (not instant or quick-cooking) oats.

Ingredients for 2 quarts
of cereal

4 cups old-fashioned rolled oats

2 cups slivered almonds

¾ cup flavorless vegetable oil

¾ cup local, unfiltered honey

4 cups dried cranberries

Special Equipment:
a parchment-lined baking sheet

Storage:

The mix will stay fresh for at least one week if stored in a sealed plastic bag or an airtight glass jar.

Adjust oven rack to the lower-middle position; preheat oven to 325° F.

1) In a large bowl, toss together the oats and almonds. Stir in the vegetable oil. Put the honey in a microwave-safe container and heat for no more than 30 seconds, just until it is pourable. Add the honey.

2) Scatter the oat mixture on the lined baking sheet, spreading it out as evenly as possible.

3) Bake until the oats and almonds turn golden-brown — 40-45 minutes. Cool on the baking sheet for one hour. Meanwhile, wash out and dry the mixing bowl.

4) Break up the chunks of granola, and put them in the cleaned out mixing bowl. Then crush the chunks with a stout wooden spoon. Gently fold in the dried cranberries.

Cinnamon-Maple Granola

This cinnamon-kissed, maple syrup-sweetened cereal will gladly perform breakfast, brunch, or dessert duty. You might like to pack it into beautiful glass jars, just as I did last December, and give it to your foodie friends for Christmas.

Ingredients for 3 quarts
of cereal

4 cups old-fashioned rolled oats

1 cup shredded coconut

1 cup sliced almonds

1 cup sunflower seeds

3/4 cup safflower oil (or use
the oil of your choice)

1/3 cup pure maple syrup

1 1/2 teaspoons ground
cinnamon

1/2 teaspoon salt

1 cup dried blueberries

1 cup dried mulberries

Special Equipment:
a parchment-lined baking sheet

Storage:

Granola will stay fresh for at
least one week in an airtight
container.

Adjust oven rack to lower-middle position; preheat oven to 325°F

1) Tip the oats, coconut, almonds, and sunflower seeds into a large bowl. Stir to combine. Then stir in the oil, maple syrup, cinnamon, and salt. Stir thoroughly to insure all ingredients are coated with the oil and syrup.

2) Scoop the granola onto the prepared baking sheet, and spread it out as evenly as possible.

3) Bake until lightly browned and fragrant – 40-45 minutes. Cool for 1 hour. Meanwhile, wash out and dry the mixing bowl.

4) Break up the chunks of granola, and put them in the clean mixing bowl. Then crush the chunks with a stout wooden spoon. Gently fold in the dried blueberries and mulberries.

Crispy Orange Juice Waffles with Roasted Strawberries

I've decided that orange juice waffles are the best waffles of all. They're crispy-crunchy outside, soft and tender inside, and fabulously infused with a sunny citrus scent. The suggested topping – Roasted Strawberries – can be made well in advance. It's a marvelous condiment not only for waffles, but for pancakes, scones, ice cream, and more.

Ingredients for 10 4-inch-square waffles

2 cups self-rising flour (see note below)

1/2 cup cornstarch

The grated zest of an orange

2 large eggs

1 3/4 cup orange juice

2 tablespoons sugar

1/2 cup neutral-tasting vegetable oil (such as safflower)

Note: If you don't have self-rising flour on hand, just whisk together 2 cups all-purpose flour, 4 teaspoons baking powder, and 1/2 teaspoon salt.

1) Preheat the waffle iron. In a large bowl, whisk together the self-rising flour, cornstarch, and orange zest. In a separate bowl, whisk together the eggs, orange juice, sugar, and oil. Tip the dry ingredients to the wet, and whisk or stir just until the flour disappears. The batter will be somewhat lumpy.

2) Ladle the batter onto the preheated waffle iron, and bake for time specified by the iron's manufacturer — usually 4 minutes.

3) Waffles are always best when served the moment they are made. In a pinch, you can keep them warm on a baking sheet in a 200°F oven. Cooled waffles can be frozen. Reheat in a 400°F oven for approximately 10 minutes.

Roasted Strawberries

Ingredients for about 2 cups

1 lb fresh strawberries, washed and hulled

1/2 cup sugar

1) Center the oven rack; preheat the oven to 450°F. Cut large strawberries into quarters, and cut small berries in half. Tip the berries into a mixing bowl, add the sugar, and toss with a spatula to coat.

2) Line a baking sheet with parchment paper. Arrange the berries in a single layer on the sheet.

3) Bake for 20 minutes, tossing the berries after 10 minutes. When the berries are cool enough to handle, transfer them to a glass jar or a plastic storage bag. Cool completely before storing in the refrigerator for up to 3 weeks.

Perfect Popovers

I think Sunday mornings were practically invented for popovers, the buttery, eggy, air-filled wonders that rise to the heavens as they bake. To eat them, you simply tear them apart and top with local honey or jam. Make the batter in an electric blender, as I do, and you and your guests can have these puffs of perfection in no time at all.

Ingredients for
6 pastries

1 1/2 cups all-purpose flour
1 1/2 cups milk
1 teaspoon kosher salt
3 large eggs
3 tablespoon unsalted
butter, melted

Special Equipment:
6 six-ounce buttered or
non-stick sprayed
custard cups

1) Adjust oven rack to the lower-middle position; preheat the oven to 425°F. Add all ingredients to the jar of an electric blender. Blend on high speed for 15 seconds. If flour sticks to the sides of the jar, scrape it down with a rubber spatula. Then blend for another 5 seconds or so.

2) Arrange the custard cups on a baking sheet. Fill each cup 2/3-full with batter.

3) Bake in the preheated oven until the pastries puff and turn golden-brown — about 40 minutes. Serve while piping hot, along with such accompaniments as butter, jam, and/or honey.

Easy-to-Peel Hard-Cooked Eggs

If you've given up on hard-cooked eggs because they are difficult to get right, I have great news for you. There is a way to achieve hard-cooked perfection each and every time: shells that come off in sheets, not shards; whites that are firm but tender, not hard or rubbery; and yolks that are golden yellow, never gray or marred by a garish green halo.

The following cooking-method has never failed me. And it works even with super-fresh, straight-from-the-hen-house eggs.

1) Use a push-pin or a special egg-piercing gadget (available at kitchen supply stores) to pierce the broad end of each shell. As the egg cooks, the tiny opening in the shell will permit air to escape, thereby reducing the chance of breakage.

2) Fill a large bowl with water and ice; set aside.

3) Set the eggs in enough rapidly boiling water to cover them by at least one inch. Then lower the heat, and let the eggs simmer – they should never actually boil – for 14 minutes. Drain off the water.

4) Working quickly now, shake the pan violently several times to encourage the shells to crack. Then *immediately* plunge the eggs into the bowl of ice water, and let them sit there for 15 minutes. The coldness will prevent a green halo from forming around the yolks. Meanwhile, as steam escapes through the cracks in the shells, the shells will pull away from the whites.

5) Peel the eggs starting at the broad end, stripping off the shells under a firm stream of tepid tap water.

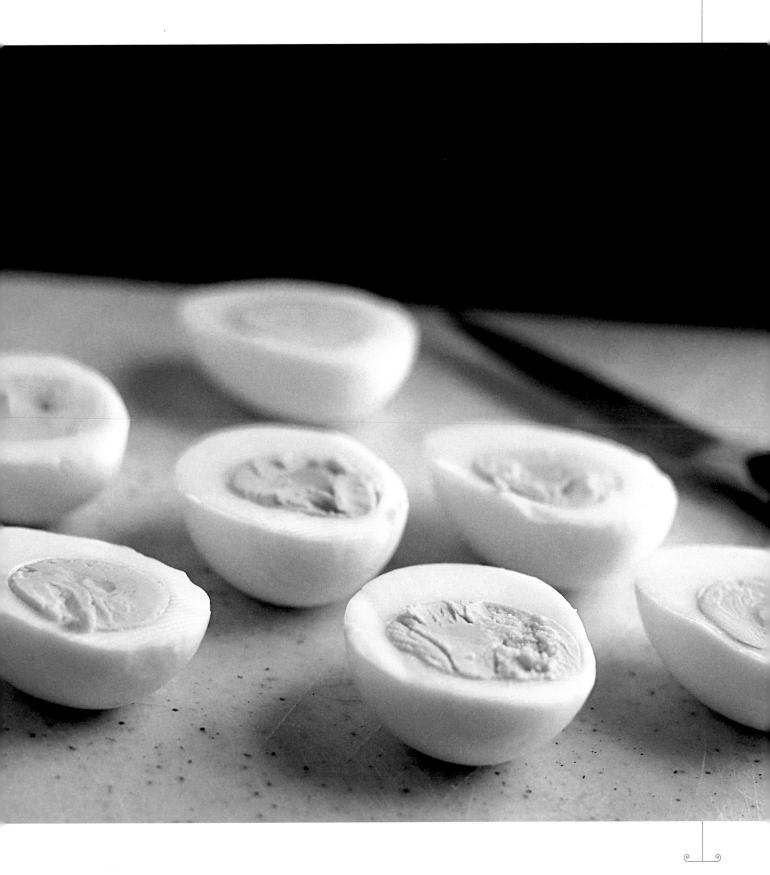

Creamy Gratin of Hard Cooked Eggs

I've made this French classic at least 500 times over the past decade. It's a symphony of hard cooked eggs baked beneath a cloak of cheesy, nutmeg-laced cream sauce. You can prepare the whole entrée the night before your brunch party, as I always do, and then pop it into the oven about half an hour before guests arrive. Serve this unabashedly rich dish with a green salad and plenty of crusty bread for mopping up the sauce, if you like.

Ingredients

Makes 4-8 servings

1 tablespoon unsalted butter
8 hard-cooked eggs, peeled (see page 18)*

2 cups half and half (or, use heavy cream)
2 tablespoons cornstarch blended with 2 tablespoons of cold water
1 cup grated Swiss cheese
1/2 tablespoon Dijon mustard
1/4 teaspoon ground nutmeg
Big pinch of salt
1/2 cup shredded or grated Asiago cheese

Special Equipment:
a buttered, 13×9-inch baking dish, and a heavy saucepan that will hold at least 2 quarts of liquid.

1) Cut the eggs lengthwise in half; arrange the halves cut-side-down in the buttered baking dish.

2) Pour the half and half or heavy cream into the saucepan, and place it over medium heat. When the liquid begins to bubble, add the cornstarch mixture. Whisk vigorously for one minute while the sauce boils and thickens. Off heat, stir in the Swiss cheese, mustard, nutmeg, and salt. Pour the sauce evenly over the eggs. Top the sauce with the Asiago cheese.

If you are not going to bake right away, cover the dish with plastic wrap, and refrigerate for up to 24 hours.

3) Center the oven rack; preheat the oven to 350°F. Bake until the sauce bubbles, and the top turns golden brown – 25-35 minutes.

Serve hot.

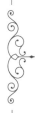

Eggs in Sweet Potato Nests

I planted some rooted sweet potato sprouts (or "slips") in my garden one spring, and the leafy vines grew like Jack's infamous beanstalk. That is, until a woodchuck turned the lot into an all-you-can-eat salad bar. Fortunately, all was not lost. When I pulled up the skeletonized vines, dozens of orange tubers revealed themselves. I used some of these beta carotene-rich subjects to make Eggs in Sweet Potato Nests — a glamorous (and gluten-free) brunch, lunch, or supper dish.

Ingredients for 6 nests (2 or 3 servings)

2 large sweet potatoes (about 2 pounds), scrubbed but not peeled

3 tablespoons vegetable oil

Kosher salt and freshly-ground black pepper

Non-stick vegetable spray (for greasing the muffin tin)

6 large eggs

For garnishing: crisp, crumbled bacon and fresh, minced parsley

Special Equipment: a muffin tin (standard or jumbo size —both types will work); a food processor OR a box grater

1) Center the oven rack; preheat the oven to 350°F. Shred the potatoes on the large-hole disk of a food processor (or use a box grater). Heat the oil in a large skillet over medium heat. Tip the potatoes into the skillet, and toss them with a generous 1/4 teaspoon of salt. Sauté the potatoes until they are tender but not mushy – about 7 minutes. Let cool for 5-10 minutes.

2) Put the muffin tin on a baking sheet, and spray 6 of the muffin openings with the vegetable spray. Scoop approximately 1/2 cup of potato shreds into each of the 6 openings, and press them, with your fingers, against the bottom and sides to create a "nest." Crack one egg into each nest, and dust lightly with salt and pepper.

3) Bake in the preheated oven until the eggs are done – 20-25 minutes. To unmold, first run a small knife around the edge of each nest. Then slip the knife under the nest, and lift up. Garnish the eggs with the crumbled bacon and minced parsley. Serve hot, warm, or even cold. Cold nests are terrific for breakfast on-the-go!

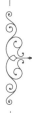

Eggs in Bacon Baskets

Eggs in Bacon Baskets are virtually carb-free. They're also easy to make, fast to bake, and chic to serve. I like to serve them on a platter lined with baby arugula for brunch, lunch, and supper parties. As with the preceding Eggs in Sweet Potato Nests, bacon baskets are terrific for breakfast on-the-go.

Ingredients for 6 baskets (2 or 3 servings)

12 strips center-cut bacon

Non-stick vegetable spray

6 large eggs

Kosher salt and freshly-ground pepper

Optional for serving: baby arugula

Garnish: finely-chopped scallion

Special Equipment: a standard-size muffin tin

1) Center the oven rack; preheat the oven to 350°F. Arrange the bacon between double thicknesses of paper towels. Microwave the bacon on "high" for exactly 2 minutes. Meanwhile, set the muffin tin on a baking sheet, and lightly coat the bottom of 6 openings with the vegetable spray. When cool enough to handle, crisscross 2 strips of bacon in each of the prepared muffin openings. Fold overhanging bacon to cover, as much as possible, the exposed sides of the openings. (Don't aim for perfection.) Crack 1 egg into each basket, and lightly sprinkle the white and yolk with salt and pepper.

2) Bake in the preheated oven until the exposed parts of the bacon turn brown and crisp, and the eggs are cooked to your liking – 20-25 minutes.

3) Run a plastic knife between bacon and muffin wall, and then slip the knife underneath the basket, and lift to unmold. For an attractive presentation, arrange the baskets on a bed of baby arugula, and garnish with the chopped scallion.

Pumpkin-Spiced Cinnamon Rolls

In my home, the joy of Christmas morning isn't complete without Pumpkin-Spiced Cinnamon Rolls. These are light, doughy, and sensually-scented with nutmeg and cloves. Serve them for breakfast, brunch, or anytime. To try them is to love them.

Ingredients for 15 rolls

For the dough:

1 packet (2 1/4 teaspoons) active dry yeast, dissolved in 1/2 cup warm (110°F) water

1/2 cup warm (110°F) milk

1/3 cup sugar

6 tablespoons unsalted butter, softened to room temperature

1 teaspoon salt

3/4 cup pumpkin puree

1/4 teaspoon ground nutmeg

Scant 1/4 teaspoon ground cloves

1/2 teaspoon ground cinnamon

3 1/2 cups all-purpose flour (plus a little more for dusting)

For the filling:

1/2 cup butter, softened to room temperature

1/2 cup sugar mixed with 1 teaspoon cinnamon

For the glaze:

2 cups confectioners' sugar blended with just enough water to make a pourable syrup

Special Equipment: 2 cake pans, 9 inches in diameter, and 2 inches deep; a standing mixer outfitted with the dough hook (or, knead the dough entirely by hand); a large, lightly-greased bowl

Preliminary step: butter the cake pans; sprinkle the entire bottom of each pan with 1 tablespoon of sugar.

1) Pour the yeast mixture into the bowl of the standing mixer. Add the milk, sugar, butter, salt, pumpkin puree, spices, and flour. Mix at low speed just until the flour is moistened – about 30 seconds. Then increase the speed to medium-high, and knead until a smooth, elastic dough develops – 4-5 minutes.

2) Scoop the dough into the large, greased bowl. Cover with plastic wrap, and let rise in a warm place until doubled in volume – about 1 1/2 hours.

3) Punch down the dough, turn it onto a lightly-floured surface, and then roll it out to form a 15- x 9-inch rectangle. Spread the dough with the softened butter, and sprinkle with the cinnamon-sugar mixture. Then roll it up tightly, beginning at the 15-inch side. Gently flatten the ends with the back of your hand.

4) Use a knife (or a piece of string) to cut the cylinder of dough into 1-inch slices. Place the slices slightly apart in the buttered and sugared cake pans. You can fit 8 slices in one pan, and 7 in the other. Set the pans in a warm place and let the rolls rise until doubled in volume – 30-40 minutes.

Meanwhile, adjust oven rack to the lower-middle position; preheat the oven to 350°F.

5) Bake until lightly-browned – 25-30 minutes. Don't over-bake, or you'll end up with crispy rolls (this isn't necessarily a bad thing). Set the pans on a wire rack, and let them cool for a few minutes.

6) Pour the confectioners' sugar into a medium bowl, and whisk in 3-4 tablespoons of water. Drizzle this glaze in between and all over the rolls. Devour with glee.

Raspberry-Goat Cheese Strata

I've made this bread pudding, or "strata" for dozens of brunch events, and it always disappears in a flash. It's a treasure trove of juicy raspberries, tangy goat cheese, and cubes of soft bread, soaked, overnight, in vanilla-scented custard. You'll find the dish is very easy to schedule for a party. Make it a day in advance, and then pop it in the oven exactly one hour before serving time.

Ingredients for 6 servings

10 slices (about 3 ounces) sandwich bread (white, whole wheat, multi-grain, or your choice), cut into 1/2-inch cubes

2 pints fresh or frozen raspberries

4 ounces goat cheese, crumbled

5 large eggs

2 1/2 cups milk or heavy cream (or, use half-and-half)

1 teaspoon pure vanilla extract

Pure maple syrup, for serving

Special Equipment:
a well-buttered 2-quart baking dish

1) Toss half of the cubed bread into the prepared baking dish. Sprinkle half of the raspberries on top, followed by half of the goat cheese. Then make a custard by whisking together the eggs, milk or cream, and vanilla extract in a medium-size bowl. Pour half of the custard over the layers of bread, berries, and cheese. Layer the remaining bread, berries, and cheese into the baking dish, and finish with the remaining custard. Cover with a sheet of aluminum foil, and refrigerate for several hours or overnight.

2) Center the oven rack, and preheat the oven to 350°F. Bake, covered with foil, for exactly 50 minutes. Then remove the foil, and continue baking until puffed and golden – about 10 minutes. Serve hot or warm with a drizzle of maple syrup.

Blueberry Streusel Strata

Here's another make-ahead casserole that will permit you to host a brunch party without breaking a sweat. It's a sonnet of blueberries and bread, nestled between layers of crisp, cinnamon-scented streusel.

Ingredients for about
8 servings

For the streusel:

2 cups "old fashioned" rolled oats

1 cup dark brown sugar

1 teaspoon cinnamon

1/4 teaspoon nutmeg

A pinch of kosher salt

4 ounces (1 stick) cold, unsalted butter, diced

For the filling:

16 ounces of sandwich bread (or a baguette), roughly torn into pieces

1 pint fresh blueberries

8 large eggs

2 1/2 cups half-and-half
(or, use plain milk)

1 cup granulated sugar

1 tablespoon pure vanilla extract

Special Equipment:
a well-buttered 9x13 baking dish;
a food processor outfitted with
the metal blade

1) To make the streusel, put the oats, brown sugar, cinnamon, nutmeg, salt, and diced butter in the bowl of the food processor. Pulse the machine until the mixture resembles coarse crumbs. Sprinkle half the streusel in the bottom of the prepared baking dish. Put the remaining streusel in a plastic storage bag, and refrigerate until baking-time.

2) To assemble the filling, put the torn bread in the streusel-lined baking dish, and top with the blueberries. Crack the eggs into a large bowl, and beat them with a wire whisk. Then whisk in the half-and-half (or milk), the granulated sugar, and the vanilla. Pour this custard over the berries and bread. Cover the baking dish with plastic wrap, and let it chill in the fridge overnight.

3) When you are ready to bake, center the oven rack and pre-heat the oven to 350°F. Then sprinkle the remaining streusel evenly over the strata, and bake, uncovered, until puffed and golden – 50 minutes to 1 hour.

CHAPTER TWO

Small Savories and Sweets for Afternoon Tea or Anytime Snacks

When life is spinning out of control, teatime can bring the whirl to a relaxing halt. The ritual of making tea the old-fashioned way (from loose leaves) always forces me to slow down and catch my breath. Even the floral pattern of my Royal Albert blue and white "Moonlight Rose" teapot is a source of calm. I purchased the pot, along with matching cups, saucers, small plates, and a three-tiered stand called an *étagère*, some twenty years ago in London. Eating and drinking from this set works almost like Xanax. I especially enjoy sharing the experience with friends.

For these occasions, I always lay the tea table with a white cloth and white linen napkins. I set the tea pot on the cloth, along with a sugar bowl and spoon (or tongs, if I am serving cubed sugar), a small pitcher of cream, a plate of thinly sliced lemons with a serving fork, small bowls for holding clotted cream and jam (if I am serving scones), a butter-knife and spoon for each guest, and, of course, tea cups and saucers.

It's easy enough to host a tea party. All you need is a pot of fragrant tea and some slices of delicious cake. Petite tea sandwiches and freshly baked scones are delightful additions for a more elaborate tea, and are surprisingly easy to make. The sandwiches can be prepared a day in advance. Scones, too, can be made ahead, and baked just before guests arrive. I'll show you my easy make-ahead techniques in the pages that follow.

Whatever you do, don't confuse an elaborate tea with "high tea." "High tea" may have a glamorous ring to it, but it is, in fact, what the nineteenth-century aristocracy referred to as the "laborer's meal," a supper where meat is always served, but tea is entirely optional.

Concerning ambience, I think a romantic setting is a must. This is the time to place fresh-cut flowers in the tearoom (which for me is usually the parlor). In addition to flowers, you might like to set potted plants on windowsills. The inclusion of so-called "Victorian" plants like African violets, or for those with more room, potted palms and Boston ferns, will make your surroundings resemble those at Kensington Palace.

I happen to know this, because I was lucky enough to enjoy afternoon tea at Kensington Palace on several occasions during the 1990s. My friend Harold Brown was butler to Princess Margaret, and whenever the Silver Fox and I were in London, he never failed to invite us to tea at his fabulous flat (next door to Charles and Diana's). It was Harold who inspired me to host teas in my own home, which I do as often as possible to this day.

No interest in Afternoon Tea? The following recipes are terrific for after-school snacking:

English Cream Scones

These are the tender, buttery pastries I enjoyed at Harold Brown's flat in Kensington Palace, and also at public venues like Richoux in Picadilly Circus, Brown's Hotel in Mayfair, and the Ritz in Paris, all sites of memorable teas. Unlike their bulky American counterparts, they do not contain dried fruit or (heaven forbid!) chocolate chips. They are plain, and plainly suited for spreading with clotted cream (or whipped cream) and jam.

Ingredients for 15
2-inch-diameter scones

2 cups all-purpose flour

1 Tablespoon
baking powder

3 tablespoons
granulated sugar

1/4 teaspoon kosher salt

6 tablespoons chilled,
unsalted butter, diced into
1/2-inch cubes

1 cup heavy cream

1 egg, beaten, for brushing
the scones

Clotted cream (p. 38) or
whipped cream, and high-
quality jam or preserves,
for serving

Special Equipment: A
food processor; a rolling
pin; a parchment-lined
baking sheet

1) Center the oven rack; preheat the oven to 425°F. Pour the flour, baking powder, sugar and salt into the bowl of the food processor; blend for 2 seconds. Remove the lid from the processor, and scatter the cubes of butter on top of the flour mixture. Replace the lid, and pulse 5-10 times just to break up the butter.

2) Transfer the flour mixture to a medium-size bowl, add the cup of heavy cream, and blend briefly with a spoon. Take care not to over-mix, or you'll end up with hockey pucks, not scones.

3) Pour the wet, sticky dough onto a lightly floured work surface. Knead 5 times — not more — and then, using a rolling pin, form the dough into a 1/2-inch-thick circle. Cut out rounds using a 2-inch diameter biscuit cutter dipped in flour. Place each round about 2-inches apart on the prepared baking sheet.

4) Lightly brush the top of each scone with the beaten egg, and then bake until the scones rise, and their tops turn lightly golden — 12-15 minutes. Cool briefly on a wire rack before serving with clotted or whipped cream and jam or preserves, if desired.

Make Your Own Clotted ("Devonshire") Cream

Clotted cream is one of life's little pleasures. It tastes like ice cream, if only ice cream could be served at room temperature. Serve this thick, rich, goodness on scones (page 36), on fruit, on pancakes, and more. Nothing could be easier to make. All you need is a quart of cream!

Ingredients for about 3 cups of clotted cream

1 quart heavy cream that has not been "ultra-pasteurized"

1) Center the oven rack, and preheat the oven to 180°F. Select a wide, shallow baking dish (such as a 2-quart casserole or gratin dish) in which the cream will not exceed a depth of more than 1 inch. Pour the cream into the dish.

2) Bake in the preheated oven until a thick yellow crust forms – about 12 hours. (If you're like me, you'll put your cream in the oven at night, or 12 hours ahead of your normal wake-up time.) Cool the cream for 30 minutes, or until it achieves room temperature. Then cover the dish with plastic wrap, and let it chill in the fridge until the cream sets up – about 4 hours.

3) Uncover the dish and then tilt it, over a bowl, to drain off some or all of the liquid. Use the liquid for coffee or baking. Scrape the thick crust (the clotted cream) into a bowl or a jar. Covered and refrigerated, clotted cream will stay fresh and wonderful for up to 4 days.

Tips for Making Tea Sandwiches

Make them in advance. Unless your household staff includes a cook named Mrs. Patmore, my advice is to make your tea sandwiches a day in advance. Just cut them into the shapes you desire, and place them on a baking sheet lined with a barely damp kitchen (or paper) towel. Cover the sandwiches with another damp towel, and then enclose the works in plastic wrap. The damp towels will keep the bread from drying out. Refrigerate for up to 24 hours.

Use thinly sliced bread. White, whole wheat, multi-grain, and gluten-free bread are all fine for tea sandwiches, *providing the bread is thinly sliced*. Pepperidge Farm "thin sliced" is acceptable, and it is available in both white and whole wheat. In any event, if you are faced with a pre-sliced loaf, and the slices are more than 1/8-inch thick, just do what my friend Harold Brown does, and flatten them with a rolling pin.

Seal the sandwich. To keep the moist filling from permeating the bread (no one wants a soggy sandwich), seal one side of each slice of bread all the way to the edges with softened butter. Cream cheese is another excellent sealant.

Remove the crusts. To show you care, always remove crusts, but only *after the sandwich has been filled*. This way, each sandwich will have clean edges.

Form small shapes. Keeping in mind that tea sandwiches should offer no more than three bites, either form them into little triangles, or, if you prefer, into rectangular "fingers." To make triangles, cut the sandwich diagonally in half. Then cut each half in half. For fingers, cut the sandwich into equal thirds.

Classic Cucumber Sandwich

You can't go wrong with this sandwich, unless you try to "modernize" it by adding surplus ingredients. The sandwich in its classic form is beloved by all. It's cool, crisp, and delicious enough for a royal tea party (so sayeth Harold Brown).

A note about cucumbers: If you have these in your garden, and they are not overgrown and therefore bitter, by all means use them for sandwiches. Remove the skin if it is either bumpy or spiky. Otherwise, use "hot house" cucumbers. These long, skinny, smooth-skinned cukes are available year-round in supermarkets and do not need to be peeled.

Another note about cucumbers. Slice them lengthwise. This is the secret to making tea sandwiches fit for a queen. Round slices are known to slip, slide, and land on laps, royal and otherwise.

Ingredients

Makes at least
9 finger sandwiches

6 slices of bread (white is traditional), buttered on one side

1 cucumber, at least 4-inches in length, peeled, if necessary

Salt and freshly ground pepper

1) Using a mandoline or a very sharp knife, cut the cucumber into paper-thin, lengthwise slices. Place two layers of cucumber on the buttered side of the bread. Sprinkle lightly with salt and pepper. Close the sandwich with another piece of bread, and press with the flat of your impeccably clean hand. Remove the crusts and cut each sandwich into three rectangles.

Smoked Salmon and Dill Sandwich

Smoked salmon. Fresh dill. Rich cream cheese. Put them on bread, and you'll have a special-occasion sandwich you can serve not only for afternoon tea, but for an elegant cocktail party, too.

Note: You can buy smoked salmon in 4-ounce packages. The long, thin slices are shaped like wings – flat on the top, and curved at the bottom. I always separate each slice to create two "wings," and then arrange them so the flat side is lined up with the edge of the bread. You'll need four individual wings for each sandwich.

Ingredients for
9 rectangles or
12 triangles

6 slices of thin-sliced
whole wheat or
pumpernickel bread

2 tablespoons cream
cheese, softened

Freshly ground
black pepper

4 ounces thinly sliced
smoked salmon

1 lemon

6 sprigs of fresh
dill, minced

1) Spread one side of each slice of bread with the softened cream cheese; dust the cream cheese with a little black pepper. Cut the salmon slices as describe in the head note, and then arrange them on one slice of bread. Give the salmon a squirt of fresh lemon and a sprinkling of minced dill.

2) Close the sandwich with another piece of bread, and press it with the flat of your hand. Remove crusts and cut each sandwich into three rectangles or four triangles.

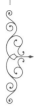

Egg and Cress Sandwich

Chopped eggs flavored with Dijon mustard and topped with peppery watercress leaves make a spicy, savory tea sandwich.

Ingredients for 12 triangles

3 slices white bread, buttered on one side

3 slices whole wheat bread, buttered on one side

2 hard cooked eggs (see my easy-peel directions, page 18)

1 teaspoon good-quality mayonnaise

1 teaspoon Dijon-type mustard

Kosher salt and freshly ground black pepper to taste

A handful of watercress leaves or baby arugula leaves

1) Thoroughly mash the hard-cooked eggs, and tip them into a medium-size bowl. Add the mayonnaise, Dijon mustard, salt and pepper, and stir until all ingredients are thoroughly combined.

2) Place one generous tablespoon of the egg mixture atop each slice of brown bread, and sprinkle on the watercress leaves. Close the sandwich with a piece of white bread, and press it with the flat of your hand. Remove the crusts and cut each sandwich into 4 triangles.

Avocado and Shrimp Sandwich

The first time I made this filling, I ate it right out of the bowl. And then I licked the bowl.
You, on the other hand, might like to save it for actual tea sandwiches.

Ingredients for
15 rectangles

1 perfectly ripe Haas
avocado, peeled and pitted

Kosher salt and freshly
ground black pepper
to taste

1 tablespoon freshly
squeezed lemon juice

2-3 drops of hot pepper
sauce (or to taste)

10 slices of bread, buttered
on one side

1 4-ounce can baby shrimp

1) In a small bowl, puree the avocado with a potato masher or a fork. Stir in the salt, pepper, lemon juice, and hot pepper sauce. Divide the mixture between 5 slices of bread, and top off with the baby shrimp.

2) Close the sandwich with another piece of bread, and press gently with the flat of your hand. Remove crusts, and cut each sandwich into 3 equal rectangles.

Marmalade Cake

Moist, tender, and fragrant, my version of this British classic contains not only marmalade, but orange juice and orange zest, too. It's really easy to make. All you need is a bowl, a whisk, and a loaf pan.

Ingredients for 1 8x4-inch loaf

3 large eggs

1 cup sugar

1 cup plain yogurt

The zest and juice of 1 large naval orange

1/4 cup orange marmalade

1/2 cup neutral-tasting vegetable (I use organic canola oil)

1 1/2 cups self-rising flour

For glazing the cake: 1 cup confectioners' sugar blended with just enough water, Cointreau, or Grand Marnier to make it pourable

Special Equipment: An 8x4-inch loaf pan, its bottom lined with a piece of parchment paper, and its sides sprayed with "baking" spray. Baking spray contains flour.

1) Center the oven rack, and preheat the oven to 350°F. In a large bowl, beat the eggs with the wire whisk. Then, one at a time, whisk in the sugar, yogurt, orange zest, orange juice (about 2 tablespoons of juice), marmalade, oil, and self-rising flour. Take care not to over mix after adding the flour – the batter should have a few lumps.

2) Pour the batter into the prepared loaf pan, and bake until puffed and golden – 55-60 minutes. Cool on a wire rack for 5 minutes; then unmold and remove the parchment paper, and place the cake on an attractive platter.

Make-ahead note: When completely cool, the cake can be wrapped in plastic, and stored in the freezer for up to 1 month.

3) In a medium bowl, whisk together the confectioners' sugar and water or Cointreau or Grand Marnier. These last two items are orange liqueurs, intended for grown-up palettes. Drizzle the glaze evenly over the top of the cake.

Serve warm or at room temperature. Try not to eat the entire cake all by your lonesome, as I have been known to do!

Victoria Sponge Cake

Take gobs of thickly whipped cream and raspberry jam, spread them between rounds of sponge cake, and what do you have? Queen Victoria's favorite teatime "sandwich."

The following sponge cake recipe comes from my mother. I love it because it produces a moist, springy, and utterly delicious cake — and involves only one bowl!

Ingredients for about
12 servings

For the cake:

2 cups all-purpose flour

1 1/2 cups sugar

3 1/2 teaspoons
baking powder

1 teaspoon salt

1/2 cup (1 stick) unsalted
butter, softened to
room temperature

1 cup milk

2 tablespoons neutral-
tasting vegetable oil, such as
organic canola

1 teaspoon vanilla

3 eggs, at room temperature
for 30 minutes

For the filling:

4-6 ounces raspberry jam (or
any preserves you like)

1 cup heavy cream,
thickly whipped

For dusting:
Confectioners' sugar

Special Equipment:
Two 9-inch cake pans; wax
paper or baking parchment
for lining the pans; an electric
hand-held mixer

1) Center the oven rack; preheat the oven to 350°F. Spray the bottom and sides of the cake pans with non-stick baking spray. Then, as further insurance against sticking, line the base of each pan with a round of parchment paper or wax paper. Give the paper a light spray.

2) Pour the flour, sugar, baking powder, and salt into a large mixing bowl; whisk briefly to combine. Then add the remaining cake ingredients. Using the hand-held electric mixer, and while scraping down the sides of the bowl with a rubber spatula, beat at low speed for 30 seconds. Then beat at high speed until the batter is smooth – about one minute. (If a spoonful of batter forms a "ribbon" when it is dripped from a spoon, you're good to go.)

3) Divide the batter evenly between the two pans. Bake until the cakes spring back when gently pressed– 25-30 minutes. Cool on a wire rack for 5 minutes. Then unmold the cakes, and peel off the paper liners. Cool completely on a wire rack before filling.

Advance preparation: The thoroughly cooled cakes will stay moist if you cover each layer with a large bowl for up to twelve hours. For longer storage, wrap the layers tightly in plastic wrap, and freeze them for up to 1 month.

4) To keep your cake platter free of confectioners' sugar, line the edge with four narrow strips of wax paper. Place one cake layer top-side down on your serving platter, then spread on the jam to within one 1/2-inch of the cake's edge. Spread the whipped cream over the jam. Place the second layer (top side up) on the whipped cream, and gently press down to spread the jam and cream to the cake's edge. Dust the cake with confectioners' sugar just before serving. After dusting the cake, pull away the strips of wax paper, and serve.

Lavender Shortbread Cookies

Last summer, I clipped several blossoms from my lavender plants and added the perfumed buds to shortbread dough. The result: a delicately floral cookie that turns any occasion into a time to stop and smell the flowers.

My version of traditional shortbread dough is as simple as simple can be, made with only butter, sugar, and flour. Additives like salt and vanilla are neither necessary nor desirable when the shortbread is scented with lavender, one of the easiest of all herbs to grow. It loves blazing sun, and poor, dry soil. *Lavandula augustifolia 'Munstead'* — the variety I have in my garden— blooms almost continually from late spring through frost. But you can choose any variety of lavender you like. All varieties are edible.

Ingredients for about
2 dozen 2-inch cookies

For the cookies:

1/2 cup granulated sugar

4 teaspoons fresh, organic lavender buds

1 cup (8 ounces, or 2 sticks) unsalted butter, softened to room temperature

2 cups all-purpose flour, scooped and leveled

For the glaze:

1 cup confectioners' sugar, blended with 1 tablespoon water

Optional decoration:

Fresh lavender buds

Special equipment: A food processor for grinding the lavender and sugar; a standing mixer; a 2-inch diameter biscuit cutter; a parchment-lined baking sheet

1) Using the food processor, grind together the lavender buds and sugar. In the bowl of a standing mixer outfitted with the paddle attachment, beat the lavender sugar and butter at low speed until smooth. Then beat in the flour at low speed until it is thoroughly combined. Mixing is complete when there are no visible lumps of butter in the dough.

2) Scoop the dough onto your work surface, and roughly form it into a disk. Wrap the disk in plastic wrap, and refrigerate for 30 minutes.

3) On a lightly floured surface, roll the shortbread into a 1/4-inch thick circle. Press out rounds with the 2-inch diameter biscuit cutter. Use a flat spatula to transfer the rounds to the lined baking sheet. Chill for 30 minute

4) Center the oven rack, and preheat the oven to 300°F Bake until the sides of the cookies begin to color – 20-25 minutes. Let cool completely on the baking sheet. Then dip the cookies in the glaze, and then let them drain on a wire rack. Decorate with a sprinkling of fresh lavender petals.

Earl Grey Cookies

These are crisp, buttery, and uniquely scented with the citrus-floral essences of Earl Grey tea leaves and rose water. Nibble slowly...and inhale deeply.

Ingredients for about
2 dozen 2-inch-diameter
biscuits

1 1/2 cups all purpose flour

1/2 teaspoon baking powder

1/2 teaspoon kosher salt

1 tablespoon Earl Grey
tea leaves

6 tablespoons unsalted butter,
softened to room-temperature

1/2 cup sugar

1/2 teaspoon pure
vanilla extract

1/2 teaspoon culinary-grade
rose water

1 large egg

Special Equipment: A food processor; a standing mixer outfitted with the paddle attachment; a parchment-lined baking sheet; a 2-inch-diameter biscuit cutter

1) Put the flour, baking powder, salt, and tea leaves in the food processor. Process until the tea leaves are finely pulverized – about 15 seconds.

2) Put the butter and sugar in the standing mixer, and beat at medium speed until light and fluffy – about 4 minutes. With the machine running at low speed, beat in the vanilla, rose water, egg, and the tea mixture. Increase the speed to medium, and beat just until the dough comes together – about 45 seconds. Enclose the dough in plastic wrap, and let it chill in the refrigerator for at least 1 hour.

3) On a lightly-floured work surface, roll the dough into a circle approximately 1/8-inch thick. Use the biscuit cutter to press out cookies, and place them 1-inch apart on the lined baking sheet. Chill for at least 15 minutes.

4) Center the oven rack; preheat the oven to 350°F. Bake in the preheated oven until the edges of the cookies feel dry – 12-15 minutes. The cookies will color only slightly. Cool them on the baking sheet for 5 minutes, then transfer to a wire rack for further cooling.

5) The cookies will stay fresh and fragrant for about 1 week if stored in an airtight container.

Autumn Spice Cookies

These are sweet, savory, crisp, and tender. The first time I made them, I ate the entire batch. Oh, the things I do for the sake of food science.

Ingredients for about
3 dozen 2-inch-diameter
cookies

2 cups all-purpose flour

2 teaspoons baking soda

1/2 teaspoon kosher salt

1 tablespoon allspice

1 teaspoon cinnamon

1 teaspoon finely ground
black pepper

12 tablespoons (1 1/2 sticks)
unsalted butter, softened to
room-temperature

1 cup granulated sugar

1/4 cup molasses

1 large, organic egg

For dusting: Superfine sugar
(about 1/4 cup)

Special Equipment:
A standing mixer outfitted
with the paddle (mixing)
attachment (or, use an
electric hand-held mixer); a
parchment-lined baking sheet

1) In a medium-size bowl, whisk together the flour, baking soda, salt, allspice, cinnamon, and pepper. In the bowl of the standing mixer, beat the butter and sugar at medium speed until light and fluffy. With the mixer running, beat in the molasses and then the egg. With the mixer running at low speed, gradually add the dry ingredients, and mix well. Cover the mixing bowl with plastic wrap, and chill in the fridge for at least one hour.

2) Center the oven rack, and preheat the oven to 350°F. Place the superfine sugar in a plastic or paper bag. Scoop up a rounded tablespoon of dough, and roll it in the palms of your hands to form a 1/2-inch diameter ball. As you work, drop each ball into the bag containing the superfine sugar. Shake the bag for a second or two. Set the sugarcoated balls 2-inches apart on the prepared baking sheet.

3) Bake until the edges of the cookies start to color — 12-15 minutes. Cool on the baking sheet for 15 minutes, and then transfer the cookies to a wire rack for further cooling.

Store the cookies in an airtight container for up to one week. For longer storage, freeze them.

But who are we kidding? Even if you live alone, these cookies won't last more than a day or two.

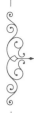

Cognac Cookies

These grown-up treats are light, buttery, and gently infused with orange-flavored cognac. They are a sophisticated addition to a Christmas cookie platter or can accompany a bowl of fresh berries in summer. They are also the perfect complement to a scoop of chocolate ice cream any time of year.

Ingredients for about 4 dozen cookies

1/2 pound (2 sticks) unsalted butter, at room temperature

1 cup confectioner's sugar (plus more for dusting)

1 egg yolk

1 tablespoon orange cognac, such as Cointreau or Grand Marnier

2 cups all-purpose flour

Special equipment: A standing mixer outfitted with the paddle attachment; a parchment-lined baking sheet

1) In the bowl of the standing mixer, beat the until perfectly smooth. Gradually beat in the rest of the ingredients one at a time, waiting to add the next until each has been incorporated: first the sugar, then the egg yolk, the cognac, and finally, the flour. Cover the bowl with plastic wrap, and refrigerate for at least 2 hours.

When you are ready to form and bake the cookies, adjust the oven rack to the lower-middle position and preheat the oven to 325°F.

2) Break off a small amount of dough, and roll it between your palms to form a 1-inch diameter ball. Place the ball on an ungreased baking sheet. Continue making balls with the rest of the dough, spacing them 1 inch apart on the baking sheet.

3) Bake until the cookies just begin to color – 20-25 minutes. Let cool on the baking sheet for 5 minutes, and then transfer to a wire rack to cool completely. Dust the cookies with the confectioners' sugar, and serve.

Chocolate Chunk Cookies with Fresh Mint

Many years ago, I planted common mint in one corner of my tiny herb garden. Can you guess what happened? The plant grew with such determination that it soon swallowed up all of my other herbs! Today, I keep this garden thug confined to a pot, where it produces just enough greenery for these refreshing chocolate-and-mint cookies.

Ingredients for about
2 dozen 2-inch-diameter cookies

1 1/2 cups all purpose flour

1/2 teaspoon salt

1/4 teaspoon baking soda

1/3 cup sugar

1/2 cup light brown sugar, packed

1/2 to 1 cup fresh, coarsely-chopped mint leaves

4 ounces (1 stick) unsalted butter, softened to room temperature

1 large egg

2 teaspoons pure vanilla extract

A 6-ounce package of semi sweet chocolate chunks (or, use 1 cup of ordinary milk-chocolate chips)

Special Equipment: A standing mixer (or, use hand-held electric beaters); a parchment-lined baking sheet

1) Whisk together the flour, salt, and baking soda in a medium bowl. In another medium bowl, combine the sugars and half of the mint. Using your impeccably clean fingers, rub the mint into the sugar until all is fragrant.

2) In the bowl of the standing mixer, cream the butter and the sugar mixture at medium-high speed until light and fluffy. Then beat in the egg, followed by the vanilla extract. At low speed, beat in the flour until it disappears into the wet ingredients. Detach the bowl from the standing mixer, and use a spatula to fold the chocolate and the remaining mint into the cookie dough.

3) Roll pieces of dough between the palms of your hands to form 1-inch-diameter balls. Space the balls 2 inches apart on the prepared baking sheet, and flatten them slightly with your fingers. Transfer the baking sheet to the refrigerate while you preheat the oven.

4) Center the oven rack, and preheat the oven to 350°F. Bake until the chocolate melts and cookies turn golden – 12 minutes for soft cookies, and 15 minutes for crisp. Cool the cookies on the baking sheet for 10 minutes, and then transfer to a rack for further cooling. When completely cool, the cookies can be stored in an airtight container for up to 3 days. For longer storage, freeze them.

Sugar Cookie Tartlets with Lemon Curd Filling

I made these for a wedding reception one year, and they wowed the crowd. To make them, you form sugar cookie dough into little cups, or "tartlets." Then you fill them with luscious, homemade lemon curd, and garnish with blueberries. Each little tart is a delectable work of art!

Ingredients for about 4 dozen tartlets

For the sugar cookie dough:

3 cups all purpose flour

1/2 teaspoon kosher salt

1 teaspoon baking soda

1 cup (2 sticks) unsalted butter, softened to room temperature

1 cup granulated sugar

2 large eggs

2 teaspoons pure vanilla extract

For the lemon curd (enough to fill 2 dozen shells)

3 large eggs

3/4 cups granulated sugar

1/3 cup freshly squeezed lemon juice

4 tablespoons (1/2 stick) unsalted butter, softened to room temperature

1 tablespoon lemon zest

For the garnish: blueberries or raspberries and mint leaves (optional)

Special Equipment: a standing mixer; a miniature muffin tin, sprayed with non-stick "baking" spray; rubber gloves to protect fingers from hot dough or a ceramic pestle.

1) Center the oven rack, and preheat the oven to 350°F. In a medium bowl, whisk together the flour, salt, and baking soda; set aside. In the bowl of a standing mixer, combine the butter, sugar, eggs, and vanilla. Beat at medium speed until light and fluffy. On low speed, gradually add the flour mixture to the butter mixture. Increase speed to medium, and beat until the ingredients are well mixed – about 2 minutes.

2) Spoon a scant tablespoon of dough into each well of the muffin tin. Bake for exactly 6 minutes. Then transfer the tin to your work surface. Using gloved fingers or a ceramic pestle (the dough will be hot), press the bottoms and sides of the dough against the walls of the muffin wells. Return to the oven for another 2-3 minutes. If the shells lose their "cup" shape, just reshape them again. They will hold up the second time around.

3) Let the tarts cool in the tin for one minute. Then unmold them, and let them cool on a wire rack. Form and bake the remaining dough. Or, wrap the dough in plastic wrap, and refrigerate for up to 3 days. For longer storage, wrap the dough well in plastic wrap and freeze for up to one month. You can freeze the baked cups, too. Just place them in a single layer in plastic zip-lock bags.

4) **For the lemon curd:** Break the eggs into a medium bowl, and beat them thoroughly with a wire whisk. Then whisk in the sugar and lemon juice. Set the bowl over a saucepan of simmering water, and whisk continually until the sauce thickens – 3 to 5 minutes. Off heat, beat in the butter and the lemon zest. Place a sheet of plastic wrap directly on the curd (it should contact the sauce to keep a skin from forming), and refrigerate for one hour or overnight.

5) Spoon or pipe the lemon curd into the cookie shell. Garnish each tartlet with a single berry. For an extra-nice presentation, stand a small mint leaf directly behind the berry.

Advance Preparation: If you are not going to serve the tartlets right away, set the filled shells on a baking sheet, cover them with plastic wrap, and refrigerate for up to 24 hours. Garnish with the blueberry and optional mint leaf just before serving.

CHAPTER THREE

Make-Ahead Cocktail Party Appetizers

When Silver Fox and I host our annual Halloween Masquerade Ball – a big cocktail party (with dancing!) to which 60-100 guests are invited – we naturally hire help. A caterer provides the finger food, a bartender pours the drinks, and then, glory hallelujah, the two of them clean up everything when the party is over. Our only jobs are to dress up like pirates, and to make sure that "Liza Minnelli," "Richard Nixon," "Liberace," and all of the other costumed guests are having a good time.

Halloween is the only large-scale event we host each year. Otherwise, our once-a-month cocktail parties are limited to just a dozen guests. The bar is self-serve. And the canapés and dips are made entirely by me.

I have a few guidelines for cocktail appetizers. They must be small, attractive, and definitely delicious. They must be safe to eat at room temperature, at least within the two-hour timeframe allotted for the party. And they must lend themselves to advance preparation. After all, I have no interest in banging around baking sheets in the kitchen while others are laughing it up in another room. I want to be a guest at my own party.

You can host a casual cocktail (or elegant New Year's Eve) party and mingle with your guests, too, if you choose your menu items from the make-ahead appetizers in this chapter.

Parsley and Parmesan Bread

This French-inspired loaf has many variations. I love it with parsley snipped right from the garden, plus shredded Parmesan cheese obtained from the supermarket. You, however, you might prefer to amend the recipe with the herbs and cheeses of your own choosing. In any event, you'll find the bread is both fast and easy to make. For a cocktail party, cut the loaf into thick slices or squares, and arrange them on an attractive platter.

Ingredients for one 8x4-inch loaf

1 generous tablespoon softened butter

Sesame seeds (for dusting the pan and topping the bread)

1 1/2 cups flour

1 tablespoon baking powder

3/4 teaspoon salt

3 large eggs

1 cup plain yogurt

1/2 cup extra -virgin olive oil

1 cup coarsely-shredded Parmesan cheese

1/2 – 3/4 cup fresh, coarsely chopped flat-leaved parsley

Special Equipment:
an 8x4-inch loaf pan

1) Center the oven rack, and preheat the oven to 350°F. Generously grease the loaf pan with the softened butter, sprinkle its bottom and sides with a tablespoon or so of sesame seeds, and set aside. In a medium bowl, whisk together the flour, baking powder, and salt. In a separate medium-size bowl, whisk the eggs. Then whisk in the yogurt, olive oil, Parmesan cheese, and parsley. Add the dry ingredients to the wet, and blend with a spatula just until the flour disappears. Do not overmix.

2) Pour the batter into the prepared loaf pan, and smooth the top with a spatula. Sprinkle the top with sesame seeds – about 1 teaspoon. Bake in the preheated oven until the loaf puffs and the top turns spotty gold – 45-50 minutes. Cool for 5 minutes in the pan. To unmold, run a knife between bread and pan. Cool the loaf on wire rack. When completely cool, the bread can be wrapped in plastic wrap and stored at room temperature for up to 3 days. For longer storage, freeze it.

Tamari Almonds

Tierra Farm in Valatie, New York, is one of my favorite Hudson Valley haunts. The farm's retail shop offers a staggering assortment of organic fair-trade coffee, as well as organic nuts and dried fruits. For cocktail parties, I buy whole, raw almonds, and roast them with tamari sauce. These slightly-salty, deep-brown crunch-ables are always a hit.

Ingredients for 1 pound of cocktail party nuts

1 pound raw, whole almonds

3 tablespoons tamari sauce

Special Equipment: a parchment-lined baking sheet

1) Center the oven rack, and preheat the oven to 350°F. Spread the almonds in a single layer on the prepared baking sheet. Roast in the oven until the nuts color – about 15 minutes. Cool for 5 minutes. Reduce oven temperature to 300°F.

2) Transfer the almonds to a medium-size bowl. Add the tamari sauce, and stir with a spoon or spatula until every nut is coated.

3) Spread the nuts in a single layer on same parchment-lined baking sheet, and roast until darkly-bronzed and fragrant – about 10 minutes.

When completely cool, Tamari Almonds can be stored for up to one month in an air-tight container.

Onion and Asiago Rounds

I make these colorful, crispy-creamy canapés for New Year's Eve
each year. I never let on how easy they are to prepare.

Ingredients for 28 canapés

28 slices of rye cocktail
bread (available in
the deli section of
most supermarkets)

1 cup good-
quality mayonnaise

Pinch kosher salt and 3
grinds of black pepper

1 small onion, minced
(about 1/3 cup)

1/3 cup minced parsley

1/3-1/2 cup finely
shredded Asiago cheese

Garnish: sliced black olives

Special Equipment:
a 2-inch diameter biscuit
cutter; a baking sheet

1) Adjust oven racks to the lower-middle and top positions; preheat the oven to 350°F.

   Using the biscuit cutter, cut the bread into 28 rounds. (Save and freeze the trimmings for stuffing or croutons). Arrange the rounds on the baking sheet and bake just until the bread dries out – about 10 minutes.

2) Meanwhile, put the mayonnaise in a medium bowl. Stir in the salt, pepper, onion, parsley, and cheese. Taste carefully for seasoning – you might want to add more salt.

Advance preparation: Let the dried out bread come to room temperature, then store in a plastic bag for up to 48 hours. Cover the mayonnaise mixture with plastic wrap, and refrigerate for up to 48 hours. Return the bread to the baking sheet when you are ready to assemble the appetizers.

3) Turn on the broiler to the "low" setting. Put a generous tablespoon of the mayonnaise mixture on each round of rye, and top with 1 or more of the olive slices. Broil just until the topping begins to brown – about 3 minutes. If you can't serve the appetizers right away, just set them on the oven's lower-middle rack, and keep them warm at 200°F.

Herbed Cheese Straws

These are crazy delicious. Think of elongated "Cheetos," kissed by the sharp tang of *real* cheddar cheese, and infused with the heavenly air of Herbes de Provence. Serve the straws at your next cocktail party, and watch them disappear. Or, just do as I did the first go-round, and eat them all by your lonesome. I'll never tell.

Ingredients for about 20 straws

1 1/2 cups shredded extra-sharp cheddar cheese

4 tablespoons (1/2 stick) unsalted butter, softened and cut into 4 pieces

3/4 cup flour

1/2 teaspoon kosher salt

1 teaspoon Herbes de Provence

1/2 teaspoon crushed red pepper flakes

1 tablespoon heavy cream

Special Equipment:
A food processor outfitted with the metal blade; a parchment-lined baking sheet

1) Center the oven rack, and preheat the oven to 400°F. Put the cheese, butter, flour, salt, herbs, and red pepper flakes in the bowl of the food processor. Pulse the machine a few times just to break up the butter. Then add the cream, and process until the dough masses on the blade – 20-30 seconds.

2) Scoop the dough onto a lightly-floured surface, and roll into a 10x8-inch rectangle, approximately 1/8-inch thick. Use a sharp, floured knife or a pastry cutter to slice the dough the long way, into 1/4- to 1/3-inch-wide strips. Space the strips 1/4-inch apart on the lined baking sheet.

3) 3Bake until the ends of the straws start to color – 12-15 minutes. Transfer to a wire rack to cool. Serve at room-temperature. Although the straws can be stored for up to 3 days in a sealed plastic bag, they are always better when served on the day you made them.

Bean Dip with Fresh Rosemary and Sage

This appetizer involves three of my favorite ingredients: creamy cannellini beans, pungent rosemary, and deep, smoky sage. It's a highly-perfumed dip that you can (and should) make a day ahead of time. Serve it with crackers or crudités.

Ingredients for about 2 cups of dip

A 15.5 ounce can of cannellini beans, rinsed and drained

1 fat garlic clove

The juice of half a lemon

1/3 cup grated Parmesan cheese

Grinds of black pepper

2 teaspoons fresh, roughly-chopped rosemary needles

7 medium-large sage leaves, roughly chopped

Olive oil

Special Equipment:
A food processor outfitted with the metal blade

1) Put the beans, garlic, lemon juice, cheese, pepper, and chopped herbs in the bowl of the food processor. Pulse the machine a few times to break up the beans and garlic. Turn the machine on, and add just enough olive oil through the feed-tube to achieve a thick, rich paste.

2) Scoop the dip into an attractive bowl, cover with plastic wrap, and refrigerate for several hours or overnight. Before serving, garnish the top with a single small sage leaf.

Cecina (Gluten-free Tuscan flatbread)

Cecina – pronounced "chay-CHEE-na" – is a Tuscan flatbread composed entirely of garbanzo bean (a/k/a "chick pea") flour, water, olive oil, and seasonings. I like to cut it into little squares or triangles for canapés, or top it with tomato sauce and cheese for pizza. It's delicious, gluten-free, and the easiest of all breads to make.

Ingredients for 1 flat bread, which can be cut into approximately 36 squares

2 1/2 cups garbanzo bean flour

3 1/2 cups cold water

1 generous teaspoon kosher salt, and grinds of black pepper

1/4 cup extra-virgin olive oil

Flavorings: a generous teaspoon of Italian seasoning blend or other dried herbs

Optional topping: 1 cup grated Parmesan or Asiago cheese

Special Equipment: a rimmed baking sheet, approximately 11x17 inches

1) In a large bowl, whisk together the flour, water, salt, and pepper. Don't worry about lumps – these will dissolve during the resting period. Cover with plastic wrap, and let sit at room temperature for 3 hours, or overnight in the fridge.

2) Center the oven rack, and preheat the oven to 350°F. Pour the olive oil (1/4 cup is not too much) on the baking sheet, and spread it evenly with a pastry brush. Give the batter a quick stir, add the herbs, and stir them into the batter. Then pour the batter onto the baking sheet, and bake until set and barely golden – about 30 minutes.

Serve as is, or top with the optional Parmesan cheese. Place under the broiler until the cheese melts – 1-2 minutes. Watch carefully to assure the bread doesn't burn.

To serve, cut the bread into 2-inch squares. If desired, cut the squares into triangles.

Variation: Cecina Pizza. Prepare and bake the flatbread as directed. Spread with your favorite pizza sauce, and top with a generous cup of shredded mozzarella cheese. Bake on the center rack of a preheated 425°F oven just until the cheese melts – 5-10 minutes. Slice and serve.

Cheese and Herb Crisps

Lily the Beagle – a/k/a "The Dairy Queen" – howls whenever I make cheese crisps.
My guests howl, too, and there are never any leftovers. They are made from nothing more than shredded cheese, and a light dusting of dried herbs or spices. And besides their value at cocktail parties, they make a terrific garnish for tomato soup.

Ingredients for
about 1 dozen crisps

6 ounces of Parmesan or
Asiago, finely shredded

Dried thyme leaves – a
small pinch for each crisp

Special Equipment:
A parchment-lined
baking sheet.

1) Center the oven rack, and preheat the oven to 375°F. Using a tablespoon, place mounds of the shredded cheese about one inch apart on the lined baking sheet. Then gently flatten each mound with the back of a spoon. Lightly dust with the dried thyme leaves.

2) Bake until the cheese colors slightly – 8-9 minutes. Cool to room temperature on the baking sheet. If you can't serve the crisps on the same day you made them, just seal them in a plastic bag. Stored at room temperature, the appetizers will retain their crispness for up to 3 days.

Chive Pesto

In March, just as the snow begins to melt, the big chive plant in my herb garden sends up lush green growth. The hollow, onion-scented stems make a fabulous pesto for dipping, spreading, and more. For cocktail occasions, either serve the pesto with plain crackers or spread it on toasted slices of a French baguette. Use any leftovers as a topping for pasta, chicken, or grilled white fish such as cod. When refrigerated, Chive Pesto will keep for up to one week in an airtight container.

Note: Use only common chives (*Allium schoenoprasum*) for this recipe. Garlic chives (*Allium tuberosum*) are too strong-tasting for pesto.

Ingredients for about 1 1/2 cups of pesto

4 cups (or more) chopped, fresh chives

2 ounces slivered almonds

1 cup freshly grated Parmesan cheese

1 garlic clove, roughly chopped

1/4 cup extra-virgin olive oil (use more or less oil to achieve the consistency you like)

Special Equipment: A food processor

1) Put the chives, almonds, cheese, and garlic into the work bowl of the food processor. Pulse just until all ingredients are coarsely pureed.

2) With the machine running, add the olive oil through the processor's feed tube to achieve the desired consistency. A quarter cup of oil will give you a spreadable sauce; add more oil to produce a pourable sauce for pasta.

Garlic Scape Pesto

Garlic scapes are the curly green shoots that emerge in summer from autumn-planted "hard-neck" garlic. Growers (like me) typically remove the shoots in order to encourage further development of the bulb below. But in recent years, garlic scapes have become a favorite of professional chefs and home cooks alike. The scapes have a distinct flavor that is potent, but without the stinging bite of a raw clove. You can find them at farmers markets from June through mid-July. One of the best uses of this powerful green I've found is in an addictive pesto. You will be serving it with *everything* once you try it.

Ingredients for about
2 cups of pesto

9-10 garlic scapes,
roughly chopped

2 ounces (1/2 cup)
slivered almonds

3/4 cup extra-virgin
olive oil

1/4 cup grated Parmesan
or Asiago cheese

Kosher salt and freshly
ground black pepper
to taste

Special Equipment:
a food processor

1) Put the scapes and almonds in the bowl of the food processor, and process until fairly smooth – about 30 seconds. Scrape down the sides of the bowl with a rubber spatula as necessary.

2) With the machine running, slowly add the olive oil, and process until incorporated – about 15 seconds. Then add the cheese, the salt, and the pepper, and blend for another 5 seconds. Taste carefully – you might like to add more salt and/or pepper. Scrape the sauce into a bowl, and then cover the bowl with plastic wrap. Refrigerate overnight for best flavor. Serve the sauce on crackers, bread, pasta, fish, chicken, and more. Garlic Scape Pesto is delicious on everything except chocolate cake.

Kale Pesto

Kale makes an exquisite pesto, especially when you infuse it, as I do, with garlic, lemon, and a whiff of nutmeg. Its culinary value isn't limited to the cracker-dipping cocktail hour. For a divine main course, the fragrant sauce can be spread on grilled chicken or baked salmon, or tossed with steaming strands of angel hair pasta for dinner. Mixed with mashed potatoes, kale pesto makes a healthy green side dish for St. Patrick's Day.

Note: If you are using large, mature leaves, you'll want to blanch them first. Blanching removes much of the leaves' natural bitterness. It also preserves their gorgeous green color. Young leaves are not particularly bitter, so you need only to blanch them if color is important to you.

Ingredients for
2 heaping cups of pesto

1 pound fresh kale leaves, the tough stems removed, and the tender green parts roughly torn or chopped

The juice of 1 lemon

4 ounces sliced (or slivered) almonds

A generous 1/2 cup grated Parmesan cheese

3 large garlic cloves

1 teaspoon (or more, to taste) kosher salt

1/4 teaspoon ground nutmeg

1/2 cup olive oil (or more, to achieve the desired consistency)

Special Equipment:
A food processor. If blanching the leaves, you'll need a large pot of boiling water; a fine-mesh sieve, a large bowl of ice water, and a terrycloth towel

1) Plunge the chopped or torn kale leaves into a large pot of rapidly boiling water, and let them cook for exactly 3 minutes. Retrieve the greens with a fine-mesh sieve, and immediately plunge them into a large boil of ice water. Chill for 3 minutes. Drain the leaves in the sieve, and then spread them out on a clean bath towel. Roll up and press down on the towel to absorb as much moisture as possible.

2) Put the blanched leaves, lemon juice, almonds, cheese, garlic, salt, and nutmeg in the bowl of the food processor. Pulse the machine several times just to break up the ingredients. Turn the machine on, and add olive oil through the feed-tube until you achieve the consistency of your dreams. Taste carefully for seasonings – you might like to add more salt and/or nutmeg.

3) When covered and refrigerated, Kale Pesto made with blanched leaves will stay fresh, colorful, and delicious for up to 5 days. Pesto made with non-blanched leaves should be enjoyed on the day of its creation.

Roasted Radish Crostini

When I was young and foolish, I thought radishes were just for slicing over salad. Now older but still foolish, I marinate and roast the red globes, and place them on ricotta-topped rounds of a baguette.

Ingredients for
2 dozen appetizers

24 common red radishes (about 1 pound), trimmed, washed and blotted dry

A generous tablespoon of olive oil

1 tablespoon honey

1 tablespoon kosher salt and grinds of black pepper

The grated zest of a lemon

The juice of half a lemon

1/2 teaspoon dried thyme leaves, plus extra for garnish

1 French baguette, sliced into 24 1/2-inch-thick rounds

1 1/2 cups ricotta cheese, stirred

Garnish: A tiny pinch of dried thyme leaves or minced fresh parsley for each crostini

Special Equipment:
A baking sheet

1) Cut each radish lengthwise in half, and then cut each half lengthwise in half to create 4 wedges. (If radishes are very small, just halve them.) In a mixing bowl, whisk together the oil, honey, salt, pepper, lemon zest, lemon juice, and thyme. Tip the radishes into the bowl, and toss with a spoon to coat. Let the radishes marinate while the oven preheats.

2) Center the oven rack, and preheat the oven to 450°F. Pour the radishes and all of their marinating liquid onto the baking sheet. Roast until radishes are tender-crisp when pierced with a small knife, their skins have blistered, and most of the liquid has evaporated from the baking sheet – about 25 minutes. Cool to room temperature on the baking sheet.

Advance preparation: When completely cool, transfer the radishes to a bowl. Cover the bowl with plastic wrap, and refrigerate for up to 2 days.

3) Thickly spread each baguette slice with ricotta cheese, and arrange 2 or 3 radishes on top. Garnish each crostini with a tiny sprinkling of dried thyme leaves or minced fresh parsley. Serve, and enjoy your party!

Variation: Raw Radish Crostini.

Slice radishes thinly, and arrange 2 or 3 slices on the same ricotta-spread bread described in the previous recipe. Garnish with chopped fresh chives and minced parsley.

CHAPTER FOUR

First-Course Soups

I like to serve a first course for dinner parties – it adds a touch of formality while prolonging the pleasure of the occasion — and soup is my usual choice. One of the best things about soup for entertaining is that it can be made a day or two in advance and then simply reheated when guests arrive.

For the sake of elegance, a first course soup should be puréed to a voluptuous consistency. And for the sake of inspiring and not sating the appetite, it should be served in small bowls, teacups, or two-handled bouillon cups. If you use large, traditional soup plates, your guests may be too full to enjoy the rest of the meal. And you can forget all about the chocolate ganache tart you planned for dessert. What a shame!

Caramelized Butternut Squash Soup

A hearty brew of caramelized squash, smoky bacon, savory thyme, and smooth sherry, this soup is a bracing way to start a fall or winter dinner party. I often serve it as the first course for Thanksgiving and Christmas dinners.

Ingredients for about 3 quarts of soup, serving 16 as a first course, and 8 as a main course

One large (4 pound) butternut squash (or two smaller ones)

2-3 tablespoons olive oil

8 slices bacon, roughly cut into 1-inch pieces

2 large yellow or white onions, peeled and chopped

1/2 teaspoon kosher salt and freshly ground black pepper to taste

A generous 1/2 teaspoon dried thyme leaves (triple the amount for fresh, chopped leaves)

5 cups low-sodium chicken stock

1/2 cup medium-dry sherry

1/3 cup heavy cream

Optional garnish: crumbled bacon, a drizzle of cream, or several droplets of pumpkin seed oil

Special Equipment:
a heavy 5-quart pot or Dutch oven; a food processor or blender for puréeing the soup

1)   Center the oven rack, and preheat the oven to 375°F. Peel the squash and cut the flesh into 1-inch cubes. Arrange the cubes on a baking sheet, coat them with the olive oil, and roast until tender and slightly colored – 50 minutes to 1 hour.

2)   While the squash is cooking, put the chopped bacon into the pot or Dutch oven. Cook over low heat until fat is rendered – about 8 minutes. Stir in the onion, salt, pepper and thyme. Cover the pot, and cook gently just until the onion is soft but not colored – about 20 minutes.

3)   Put the bacon mixture and one cup of the chicken stock into the food processor or blender, and blend until perfectly smooth – about 30 seconds. Quickly wash out and dry the soup pot. Return the puréed mixture to the pot.

4)   Pour the cooked squash and one cup of chicken stock into the food processor or blender (you needn't clean these out first), and process until smooth. Pour the puréed squash into the pot.

5)   Add the remaining 3 cups of chicken stock to the pot. Stir in the sherry and the cream. Bring to a boil, and then reduce the heat. Let simmer uncovered for 10 minutes.

Advance preparation: If you are not going to serve the soup right away, let it cool to room temperature. Then refrigerate, covered, for up to 4 days. When you are ready to serve, bring the soup to a simmer, and stir in a little extra cream.

To serve, ladle the soup into bowls. Garnish each serving with crumbled bacon and/or a drizzle of cream

Soupe a l'Ail
Garlic Soup

Don't be put off by the name of this French soup. It's actually as suave and mellow as a James Taylor ballad. To make it, you simmer garlic, herbs, and cloves in water. Then you strain the fragrant broth, and thicken it with egg yolks. Served with toasted rounds of a baguette, and sprinkled with shredded Asiago cheese (I pass the cheese in a bowl, and let guests serve themselves), the soup makes a fine first course for dinner.

Ingredients for 2 1/4 quarts of soup, or enough for 8 servings as a first course

For the broth:

2 big heads of garlic, the individual cloves smashed but not peeled

3 whole cloves (the spice)

2 teaspoons kosher salt, and freshly ground black pepper to taste

1/4 teaspoon dried thyme (triple the amount for fresh)

4 large sage leaves, roughly chopped

1 bay leaf (preferably Turkish)

6 sprigs flat-leaf parsley

3 tablespoons olive oil

2 quarts water

For thickening the soup:

3 egg yolks

1/4 cup olive oil

For garnishing the soup:

2 tablespoons fresh, minced parsley

1 cup shredded Asiago cheese

Special Equipment:
A 3-quart saucepan with a lid; a fine mesh sieve

1) Put all of the broth ingredients into the saucepan, and bring to a boil over high heat. Then reduce the heat, cover the pan, and let simmer quietly for 30 minutes.

2) Set the sieve over a large bowl. Strain the broth through the sieve, pushing down on the ingredients with the back of a big spoon to help extract their juices.

Advance preparation: If you are not serving the soup right away, let the strained broth cool to room temperature. Then cover and refrigerate for up to 3 days. Reheat the broth before continuing with the recipe.

3) In a separate bowl, violently beat the egg yolks until they turn pale and thick – about 30 seconds. Whisking constantly, add the olive oil in slow, steady steam to form a thick, rich, mayonnaise-like sauce.

4) Pour the egg mixture into a soup tureen or serving bowl. Whisking vigorously, add one 1/2 cup of the hot broth to the egg mixture. Then whisk in the remaining broth, and stir in the minced parsley.

To serve, ladle the soup into bowls or cups. Put the shredded cheese in a small, attractive bowl, and pass it at the table.

Leek and Potato Soup

I first learned about leeks at age 14, when Juliette Miller – a school friend's French-born-and-raised mother – gave me a paper bag filled with the fat, pale-green stalks, freshly dug from her garden. When I asked what I should do with them, Juliette took a pencil from her purse, and scribbled on the bag a recipe for Leek and Potato Soup. I made the soup the next day, and immediately fell in love with its mild onion flavor and velvety consistency.

You can serve Leek and Potato Soup either hot or cold. Served cold, it is known (in America, anyway) as *Vichyssoise*. Served in a small bowl or a two-handled cup, it's an irresistible starter for a luncheon or dinner.

Ingredients for 6-8 servings as a first course, or 4 servings as a main course

4 tablespoons (1/2 stick) unsalted butter

4-5 large leeks, white and pale green parts only, rinsed and roughly diced

1 tablespoon kosher salt, and freshly ground black pepper to taste

6 cups hot (or boiling) water

1 1/2 tablespoons cornstarch blended with 1/4 cup *cold* water

1 1/2 pounds (about 2 medium) Yukon Gold potatoes, peeled and coarsely diced

1 cup milk or cream, or a combination of the two

Suggestions for garnish:
A drizzle of cream, a sprinkling of minced parsley, and – if you are not passing a loaf of bread at the table — some small croutons for each serving

Special Equipment:
A heavy pot or Dutch oven that will hold 4-5 quarts; a blender, food processor, or immersion blender for puréeing the soup

1) Put the butter in the pot, and let it melt slowly – it shouldn't color at all – over low heat. Then stir in the diced leeks, salt, and pepper. Cover the pot and let the leeks sweat until perfectly tender – 10-20 minutes.

2) Cover the leeks with the hot or boiling water. Turn up the heat, add the cornstarch mixture, and stir slowly and constantly until the liquid bubbles and thickens – about 1 minute.

3) Add the potatoes, lower the heat, and partially cover the pot. Let simmer quietly for 25-30 minutes, or until the potatoes are definitely tender. Purée the soup to a smooth consistency.

Garnish each serving with cream, minced parsley, and optionally, some small, crisp croutons

Variation: Watercress Soup. Bring the finished Leek and Potato Soup to a simmer. Add 1 bunch of watercress. Stir until the stems and leaves wilt – about 1 minute. Purée the soup.

Lettuce Soup

It's a shame that most folks only think of lettuce as a cold salad component. In fact, its true calling is soup! All dark-green lettuce varieties (including spinach) are suitable for soup-making. The following recipe produces a tangy, tantalizing brew. I just love it.

Ingredients for about 2 quarts of soup, or enough for 8 servings as a first course

1 tablespoon unsalted butter

1 tablespoon extra-virgin olive oil

1 large white onion, roughly chopped

2 large garlic cloves, peeled and roughly chopped

1 teaspoon kosher salt

2 large russet potatoes (1 1/2 pounds), peeled and roughly diced

6 cups unsalted chicken stock

1 teaspoon dried thyme leaves (triple the amount for fresh leaves)

2 heads of romaine lettuce or another dark, leafy green (about 2 pounds)

10 chive stems, roughly chopped

The juice of half a lemon

1 1/2 cups sour cream (or Greek yogurt)

Freshly-ground black pepper

Finely-chopped chives and small, crisp croutons for garnish

Special Equipment:
A heavy, 5 quart soup pot or Dutch oven; a food processor, blender, or immersion blender for puréeing the soup

1) Over low heat, melt the butter with olive oil in the pot or Dutch oven. Stir in the onion and salt, and then cover the pot, and let the onion sweat until soft – about 5 minutes. Stir in the garlic, salt, potatoes, chicken stock, and thyme. Bring to a boil over high heat, and then cover the pot, lower the heat, and let simmer quietly until the potatoes are tender – about 30 minutes. Add the chives and the lettuce leaves. Use a large spoon to push the leaves down into the hot liquid so they will wilt. Off heat, stir in the lemon juice and sour cream.

2) Purée the soup to a thick and creamy consistency. Then transfer the purée to a large serving bowl or tureen, and stir in several grinds of black pepper. Taste carefully for seasonings — you might like to add more salt. If you are not serving the soup right away, let it cool to room temperature. Then cover and refrigerate for up to 3 days.

Serve the soup hot in winter or cold in summer, garnished with finely-chopped chives and small, crisp croutons. The soup will convince you that lettuce isn't just for salads!

Red Bell Pepper Soup

This colorful concoction was inspired by produce from my late-summer garden. It's scented with thyme, thickened with russet potatoes, and subtly sweetened with red bell peppers. Smashed garlic cloves provide just the right amount of zing. You can find all of the ingredients at your local supermarket, so you can enjoy this soup year-round.

Ingredients for about 2 quarts of soup; enough for 8 servings as a first course

2 tablespoons unsalted butter

2 tablespoons olive oil

1 large yellow onion, peeled and roughly chopped

4 red bell peppers, roughly diced

2 large russet potatoes (1 1/2 pounds), peeled and roughly diced

5 garlic cloves, smashed and peeled

2 teaspoons dried thyme leaves (triple the amount for fresh)

2 teaspoons kosher salt and freshly ground black pepper to taste

3 cups (or slightly more) low- or no-sodium chicken stock

Sour cream, yogurt, or crème fraîche, and a sprinkling of minced chives or dill, for garnish

Special Equipment:
A heavy-bottom 5-quart pot with a lid; a food processor, a blender, or an immersion blender for puréeing the soup

1) Heat the butter and oil in the pot over a low flame. When the butter melts, add the onion, bell peppers, potatoes, garlic, thyme, and salt and pepper. Briefly stir to coat all vegetables with the butter and oil. Cover the pot and let the vegetables steam until perfectly tender – 50-60 minutes. Remove the lid and let cool for 10 minutes.

2) Using an immersion blender, purée the vegetables directly in the pot. Or, purée them in 2-cup batches in a blender or food processor, and then transfer the finished batches to a large bowl. If you use a blender of food processor, rinse out the large pot before returning the purée to the pot.

3) Stir 3 cups of chicken stock into the puree, and bring to a simmer over a medium flame. If the soup is too thick for your liking, add a little more stock. Taste carefully for seasonings.

To serve, ladle the soup into bowls or cups. Top each serving with a dollop of sour cream, crème fraîche, or yogurt and a pinch of minced chives or dill.

Carrot-Ginger-Orange Soup

You don't have to serve this soup as the first course for dinner. The flavor combo of carrots, ginger, and orange juice is welcome any time of the day. Pour the soup into a mug, and enjoy it for breakfast, lunch, or whenever you need a beta carotene pick-me-up.

Ingredients for about 2 quarts of soup

1 tablespoon unsalted butter

1 tablespoon olive oil

1 large onion, peeled and roughly chopped

2 fat cloves of garlic, peeled and roughly chopped

18-20 large carrots, peeled and roughly chopped

1 teaspoon kosher salt (or more, to taste)

6 cups unsalted chicken stock

The juice and grated zest of 1 large navel orange

1 tablespoon freshly-grated ginger

A generous splash (1/4-1/2 cup) heavy cream

Garnish: A dollop of Crème Fraîche and a pinch each of orange zest and minced, fresh parsley for each serving

Special Equipment:
A 5-quart pot or Dutch oven with a lid; an electric blender or immersion blender for puréeing the soup

1) Warm the butter and olive oil in the pot over low heat. When the butter melts, stir in the onions. Then cover the pot, and let the onions cook until translucent (they must not color at all) – about 8 minutes. Add the garlic, carrots, salt, and chicken stock. Bring to a boil over high heat. Then reduce the heat, cover the pot, and let simmer until the carrots are perfectly tender – about 30 minutes.

2) With the help of an immersion blender or a regular blender, purée the soup to a smooth consistency. Then transfer the soup to a large serving bowl or tureen, and stir in the orange zest, grated ginger, and heavy cream. Taste carefully for seasonings – you might like to add more salt.

Serve the soup hot, warm, or cold, garnishing each serving with a dollop of Crème Fraîche and a small pinch of orange zest and minced parsley.

CHAPTER FIVE

Main Courses for Simple Suppers and Divine Dinners

My Top Ten Tips for Hosting a Successful Dinner Party:

1. Keep the guest-list small. I think 4-6 guests are ideal. For a larger party, consider paying for qualified help. You'll find the money is well spent.

2. Refuse help from guests, even when they offer. Several years ago, I caved and let a guest wash some of my prep dishes. Can you guess what happened? He took a steel wool soap pad, and ferociously scoured my cast-iron skillet. Ten years of the pan's acquired non-stick patina – gone! Lesson learned.

3. Prepare ahead. Do what I do, and select a menu that can be mostly – if not entirely – made in advance. This way, you can relax and enjoy your party. Keep in mind that guests feel uncomfortable around a harried host. And even worse, they offer to help. (See Tip #2.)

4. Set the table and polish the silver. Accomplish these jobs well-ahead of your party. There's nothing worse than discovering a wrinkled tablecloth and horribly tarnished flatware just before your guests arrive.

5. Is your lighting inviting? Dim the overhead lights, or dine by candlelight. Trust me, everyone glows in candle glow!

6. Use the fireplace. If you have a fire-place in your dining room, by all means light it for winter-time dinner parties. The flames will both warm and brighten the room, and everyone will remember the romantic atmosphere you created.

7. Put flowers on the table. Unless you have a soup tureen in the center of the table, place a low bouquet there. Avoid highly-scented blooms, as they will inter-fere with the aromas of your courses. Chrysanthemums offer no scent, and they are both beautiful and long-lasting.

8. Seating. Position the most engaging talkers across from each other, along the middle of the table. This will reduce the risk of separate, and often quite loud, conversations at opposite ends of the table.

9. Never apologize. I learned this tip from Julia Child. If the food you prepared is not up to your usual standards, don't bring these facts to your guests' atten-tion. Nobody likes an unsatisfied cook.

10. Remember the 1 hour rule. If you ask guests to arrive for drinks at 7:00PM, be prepared to serve dinner at 8:00PM. Guests who have to wait longer than one hour to dine will definitely gorge them-selves on the cocktail appetizers you provided. As a result, few will appreciate your dinner, no matter how enticing the food may be.

Tomato Pie

Tomato Pie is the best reason I know for growing heirloom tomatoes, or at least for buying them in season from local farm stands. The few ingredients come together to make something much greater than the sum of the parts: tender, flakey biscuits, luscious juicy tomatoes, and rich and unctuous mayonnaise and cheese. The pie is extremely easy to make, especially if you cheat (as I do) and use store-bought biscuits for the crust.

Wine pairing: Bandol Rouge or Syrah

Ingredients for 4 generous servings

10 biscuits (from a 7.5 ounce package)

2 large, perfectly ripe tomatoes, sliced 1/4-inch thick

Kosher salt and freshly ground black pepper

10 or more large, fresh basil leaves

1 cup mayonnaise

1 cup shredded, extra-sharp cheddar cheese

Special Equipment:
a 9-inch pie plate, lightly buttered or sprayed with vegetable spray

1) Center the oven rack, and preheat the oven to 375°F. Press the biscuits against the bottom and sides of the pie plate, making sure there are no gaps in the crust. Layer the tomato slices on top of the dough, and give them a sprinkling of salt and pepper. Stack the basil leaves, and then tightly roll them from tip-end to stem-end as if you were rolling a cigar. Slice cross-wise into thin strips, and scatter over the tomatoes.

2) In a small bowl, blend the mayonnaise and cheese together. Place big dollops of the cheese mixture on top of the tomatoes and basil, and then spread it around with the back of a spoon (or, use an offset spatula) to cover the pie evenly.

3) Bake until puffed, golden, and fragrant – 30-35 minutes. To assure a firm, not runny pie, let rest for 30 minutes before serving.

Chicken and Lemon Polpettine

These Old-World Italian meatballs (which we should never confuse with "American" meatballs) are flavored with Parmesan cheese, fragrant herbs, and a big burst of lemon. I like to serve them on a platter of baby arugula leaves, or, for a heartier meal, on a bed of warmed cannellini beans. They do not require a sauce of any kind.

Wine suggestion: Alsace Pinot Gris

Ingredients for about
20 1-inch diameter
meatballs – enough for 4
servings

1 pound ground chicken

1 1/4 cups
fresh breadcrumbs*

Juice and zest of one lemon

1 teaspoon kosher salt (more
or less to taste) and freshly
ground black pepper

1/4 cup (or slightly more) fresh,
minced flat-leaf parsley

1 generous teaspoon
dried thyme leaves (triple
this amount for fresh,
chopped leaves)

1/4 cup finely grated Parmesan
(or Asiago or Romano) cheese

1/3 cup flour for coating
the meatballs

2 tablespoons olive oil

3 tablespoons unsalted butter

*To make fresh breadcrumbs, simply
tear up some fresh sandwich-
type bread, and grind it up in a
food processor. Leftover crumbs
will freeze perfectly well in an
airtight bag.

Special Equipment:
a large skillet (or an electric
skillet heated to 350°)

1) Put the ground chicken in a large bowl. Add the breadcrumbs, lemon juice and zest, salt, pepper, parsley, thyme, and cheese, and mix them all together with perfectly clean hands.

Advance preparation: The chicken may be prepared to this point, and then covered and refrigerated for up to 24 hours.

2) Pour the flour into a pie plate. Form tablespoon-size balls of the chicken mixture, flatten them slightly (for faster cooking), and then dredge them in the flour on both sides.

3) Heat the oil and butter in the skillet. When the butter has melted and the foam subsides, fry the polpettine until crusty and golden brown – 4-5 minutes (or slightly longer) per side.

Serve at once, or keep warm on a baking sheet (uncovered) for up to 30 minutes in a 200° oven.

A Simple Supper of Sausages, Cabbage, and Sweet Potato

This assembled dish contains three of my wintertime favorites — tender-crisp cabbage, bronzed sausages, and orange coins of sweet potato. It's a perfect meal for the low-carb crowd.

Ingredients for at least
3 servings

6 sweet "Italian"
sausages (or,
substitute Bratwurst)

Olive oil

1/2 large head green
cabbage, finely shredded

Seasonings: a generous
sprinkling of salt and
freshly-ground black
pepper, and 1 teaspoon
fennel seeds

1 large sweet potato
(about 1 1/2 pounds),
scrubbed and sliced into
1/4-inch-thick rounds

Special Equipment:
a shallow roasting pan
with a rack; a 9x13
baking/serving dish

1) Center the oven rack, and preheat the oven to 425°F. Put the sausages on the rack in the roasting pan, and brush their tops with a thin layer of olive oil. Roast in the preheated oven until the sausages are done, and the casings are brown and crisp – 35 minutes.

2) Meanwhile, preheat a large skillet over medium heat. Pour a glug of olive oil into the hot skillet, add the cabbage, salt, pepper, and fennel seeds, and toss to coat. Then cover the skillet, and cook until the cabbage is tender-crisp – about 5 minutes.

3) While the cabbage is cooking, put the sweet potato slices and 1/4 cup water in a glass bowl. Cover the bowl tightly with plastic wrap. Microwave on "high" until the slices are tender but not mushy – 5-6 minutes. Drain the slices, and give them a light dusting of salt and pepper.

4) Pour the cabbage into the baking dish, and spread it out evenly. Top with the sausages, and arrange the sweet potato coins all around the perimeter of the dish. Serve at once, or keep warm in a 200°F oven for up to 30 minutes.

Gobble-Gobble Squash

Last autumn, just for fun, I roasted a quartet of acorn squash. Then I filled the cavities with a simple sauté of ground turkey, tomato paste, Worcestershire sauce, red wine, fragrant thyme, and a flurry of Parmesan cheese. The final product, which the Silver Fox and I devoured before a roaring fire, seemed to capture the very essence of autumn. The only problem? What to name the dish. Gobble-Gobble Squash seemed appropriate, because...ground turkey. Substitute ground beef, and I suppose you can call the dish "Moo-Moo Squash."

Wine suggestion: Cabernet Sauvignon

Ingredients for
4 servings

For the squash:

4 small acorn squash

2 tablespoons melted butter

For the filling:

1 1/2 pounds ground turkey breast

1 generous tablespoon olive oil

1 large onion, finely minced

1/2 cup dry red wine (such as Cabernet Sauvignon)

1 1/2 teaspoons Worcestershire sauce

6 ounces plain tomato paste

Salt and freshly-ground pepper to taste

1 teaspoon dried thyme leaves

1 tablespoon cornstarch blended with just enough water to make a thick paste

Shredded Parmesan cheese – a generous pinch for each squash

Special Equipment:
A baking sheet and a large non-stick skillet

1) Center the oven rack, and preheat the oven to 425°F. To insure the squash will stand up straight, slice off the little point located at the blossom end of the squash. Then slice off a "lid" from the stem end, just as you would for a jack-o-lantern. Save the lids. Plunge a soup spoon into the exposed flesh, scraping down and around to remove fibers and seeds. Stand the squash upright on a baking sheet, and brush the exposed flesh and cavities with the melted butter. Arrange the lids on the baking sheet, but do not butter them. Roast until the flesh is definitely tender when pierced with a fork – about 40 minutes.

2) Meanwhile, over medium heat, brown the ground turkey in the skillet, breaking up the meat with a wooden spoon or spatula as it cooks. Transfer the finished turkey to a bowl, and set aside. Add the olive oil and the minced onion to the skillet. Then lower the heat, cover the skillet, and let the onions sweat until tender – about 5 minutes. Then increase the heat, and stir in the wine, Worcestershire sauce,

tomato paste, salt, pepper, and thyme. Stir for 1 minute while the mixture bubbles. Then stir in the cold cornstarch solution, and remove the pan from the heat.

3) Spoon the filling into the squash cavities, and top with a generous pinch of the Parmesan cheese. Bake in the hot oven just until the cheese melts – 5-10 minutes. Plate the squash with the lids arranged on top, and serve. The only accompaniment the squash requires is a bottle of Cabernet Sauvignon. Cheers!

Chicken Thighs en Papillote

This is my go-to dinner when I need to lose a few pounds. It's an inexpensive, low-carb meal of fresh green beans, boneless chicken thighs, plus onions, garlic, and herbs, all steamed to aromatic awesomeness in a parchment package. Although the ingredients listed below are for just one serving, you can certainly make extra packages for guests. It's a *company-worthy* diet dish!

Wine suggestion: Sauvignon Blanc

Ingredients for 1 serving

A handful (about 4 ounces) fresh green beans, trimmed

1/4 cup chopped onion

1 garlic clove, minced

Olive oil

Kosher salt and freshly ground pepper

1/8 teaspoon dried thyme leaves

Dry French vermouth – a small splash

2 skinless, boneless chicken thighs (each weighing about 4 ounces)

1/4 teaspoon dried tarragon leaves

Garnish: 1 tablespoon finely chopped flat-leaf parsley

Special Equipment:
A sheet of parchment paper, approximately 15x20 inches; a baking sheet

1) Center the oven rack, and preheat the oven to 400°F. Place the parchment paper on the baking sheet. Center the beans, and top them with the onion and garlic. Give the veggies a drizzle of olive oil, a sprinkling of salt, pepper, and thyme, and a short splash of vermouth. Place the chicken thighs on top of the veggies, and dress them with a little olive oil, a tiny pinch of salt and pepper, and the tarragon leaves.

2) Draw up the two long ends of paper, and fold them to seal. Do not fold all the way down to the chicken, because there must be air space in order for steam to develop. Fold the two ends of the package, and press firmly to seal.

3) Bake until the beans are tender-crisp and the chicken is tender, succulent, and thoroughly cooked – 35 to 40 minutes.

To serve, unfold the parchment. Then slip a wide, flat spatula under the beans, and slide the works onto a plate. Garnish with the chopped parsley.

Turkey-Carrot-Bacon Loaf

Call me a dirty freakin' hippy, but I favor ground turkey – not ground beef — for meatloaf. And to make the poultry sing, I enrich it with shredded carrots, chopped parsley, and Worcestershire sauce. The hot, savory slices are terrific for dinner, with such accompaniments as lightly-dressed baby arugula leaves and Creamy Mashed Potatoes (see the following recipe and its variations). Cold, leftover slices are sensational for sandwiches.

Wine suggestion: Pinot Noir

Ingredients for one 9x5-inch loaf (about 8 servings)

2 lbs ground turkey

3 fat carrots, shredded

1 cup fresh, coarsely-chopped parsley

1/2 teaspoon kosher salt, and several grinds of black pepper

2 large eggs, beaten

A generous tablespoon of Worcestershire sauce

1 cup fresh (not dried) bread crumbs

3/4 cup shredded, extra-sharp Cheddar cheese

6 ounces tomato paste

3 strips bacon (center-cut preferred)

Special Equipment:
A lightly-greased 9x5-inch loaf pan

1) Center the oven rack, and preheat the oven to 350°F. In a large bowl, thoroughly combine the turkey, carrots, parsley, salt, pepper, eggs, Worcestershire sauce, bread crumbs, and cheese. Transfer the mixture to the lightly-greased 9x5-inch loaf pan, and pack it down evenly. Top with the tomato paste and strips of bacon.

2) Bake in the preheated oven until the internal temperature reaches 165°F – 60-65 minutes. Cool for 10 minutes before slicing.

Creamy Mashed Potatoes

These are everything you'd want them to be: rich, buttery, and sinfully delicious.
For the best texture, mash the spuds by hand.

Ingredients for about 8 servings

4 pounds starchy potatoes (i.e., 'Kennebec' or 'Russet')

1/2 cup (1 stick) melted butter

1/2-3/4 cup heavy cream

Salt and freshly-ground black or white pepper to taste

Special Equipment:
a 5-quart pot or Dutch oven; a potato masher

1) Peel the potatoes, and then roughly cut them into equal-size pieces. Immediately plunge the cut pieces into a large (5 quart) of cold water to stop them from coloring. Bring to the pot to a full boil over high heat. Then lower the heat, partially cover the pot, and simmer until the potatoes are absolutely tender when pierced with a fork (you should feel no pressure against the fork) — 30 minutes or slightly longer.

2) Drain the potatoes, and then return them to the cooking pot. Set the pot over medium heat, and roughly mash the spuds with a common potato-mashing gadget. Mashing over heat will permit excess moisture to evaporate from the spuds. Off heat, mash in the butter, followed by the cream. Use enough cream to achieve a soft, thick consistency. Mash in the salt and pepper. Taste carefully to correct seasonings, and serve while hot.

Variation 1: Parsley Mashed Potatoes. After the butter, cream, and seasonings have been added to the mash, stir in 1 cup finely-minced parsley.

Variation 2: Pesto Potatoes. To the finished mashed potatoes, stir in 1/2 cup (or more, or less) of any of the pesto varieties listed in Chapter 3. Not only will the pesto add intense flavor to the potatoes, but it will turn them green for St. Patrick's Day!

Zoodles and Yoodles with Garlic

What inspired this vegetable "pasta" dish? A small, hand-held gadget known as the "julienne peeler." The peeler turns zucchini into thin noodle-like strips, or "zoodles." Use it to peel yellow squash, and you'll have "yoodles." Sautéed in olive oil, these zoodles and yoodles have a similar texture to spaghetti. For a lightning-fast meal, I simply top the squash with minced parsley, Romano cheese, small basil leaves, and slivered almonds. Then I eat chocolate cake for dessert.

Ingredients for 1 large (or 2 modest) servings

2 zucchini, each no longer than 8 inches in length

2 yellow squash, 5-8 inches in length

2 tablespoons unsalted butter

1 tablespoon olive oil

2 cloves of garlic, minced

Kosher salt and freshly-ground pepper – a generous pinch of each

Garnish: fresh, minced parsley, grated Romano cheese, baby basil leaves, halved cherry tomatoes, and slivered almonds – a small handful of each

Special Equipment: a julienne peeler

1) Slice off the stem and blossom ends of the zucchini and yellow squash. Use the julienne peeler to peel the squash until you reach the seed-filled cores. (Save the cores for soup or raw eating.)

2) Warm the butter and oil in a skillet set over medium heat. When the butter melts, add the garlic, and sauté for 15 seconds. Then add the squash, and sauté until just heated through – about 2 minutes.

Divide the squash between 2 plates, and garnish with the parsley, Romano cheese, basil leaves, cherry tomatoes, and almonds. Serve immediately.

Pâte Brisée for Savory Tarts

For the savory tarts that follow, my crust of choice is tender, buttery Pâte Brisée (pronounced "pat bree-ZAY"). With the help of a food processor, you can make this classic French pastry dough in about a minute.

"But Kevin," you say, "why can't I use commercial, 'ready-made' pie crust for my savory tarts?"

I'm so glad you asked.

Ready-made pie crust from the supermarket might be convenient to use, but it tastes like the cardboard box in which it is sold. If flavor, texture, and bragging rights are important to you, then by all means make Pâte Brisée.

Ingredients for 1 crust

1 1/2 cups all-purpose flour

1/2 teaspoon salt

8 tablespoons cold, unsalted butter, cut into a 1/2-inch dice*

3 tablespoons (or more) ice water

*To dice the butter, first cut the stick lengthwise into quarters. Then cut the quarters crosswise into 1/2-inch cubes.

Special Equipment:
a food processor

1) Put the flour and salt in the work bowl of a food processor, and give them a 2-second spin just to combine. Remove the lid from the machine, and scatter the cubes of butter on top of the flour. Then replace the lid, and pulse 10-15 times, just to break up the butter.

2) With the machine running, quickly add the ice water through the feed-tube. Process until the dough begins to mass on the blade. Then test the dough: if it holds together when pressed between your fingers, it's ready to go. If the dough is too dry to hold together, simply pulse in 1 or 2 additional tablespoons of ice water.

3) Pour the crumbly mass onto a non-porous work surface (I use a marble slab), and form it into a ball. Then flatten the ball into a disk, wrap it in plastic wrap, and refrigerate for at least 30 minutes in order to firm up the butter.

Pâte Brisée can be refrigerated for up to 2 days, or frozen for up to 3 months.

Variation: Pâte Brisée Sucrée. This is the sweet French pastry dough you'll need for rustic fruit tarts, such as the Blueberry Galette on page 176. Simply add 2 tablespoons of sugar to the ingredients listed for savory Pâte Brisée.

Ham, Kale, and Swiss Cheese Tart

I'm not quite sure when or how kale became everyone's favorite vegetable, but there are good reasons for its newfound star power. It's as healthy as a vegetable can be, it can be eaten raw or cooked in innumerable ways, and it tastes great. In this recipe, blanched kale, smoky ham, and mellow Swiss cheese are featured players in a rustic savory tart, while nutmeg and vermouth play subtle supporting roles. Serve it with a green salad any time of the year, and enjoy the applause.

Wine suggestion: Beaujolais

Ingredients for 4 servings

For the filling:

1 tablespoon olive oil

1 tablespoon unsalted butter

1/2 pound (or slightly more) fresh kale

1 large white onion, diced

1 cup (or slightly more) cubed, cooked ham

Salt and freshly ground pepper to taste

1/8 teaspoon ground nutmeg

2-3 tablespoons dry French vermouth

For the crust:

Pâte Brisée (see the recipe on page 124)

For the cheese base:

1 cup ricotta cheese, blended with 1/2 cup shredded Swiss cheese

For topping the tart:

A handful (about 1/2 cup) shredded Swiss cheese

Special Equipment:

A rimless, 15 x 14-inch (or larger) baking sheet (or use a rimmed baking sheet turned upside down), lightly buttered or sprayed with vegetable spray; a large pot of boiling water for blanching the kale; a clean kitchen towel for squeezing the kale; a colander or a wire-mesh strainer

Note: The first step of this recipe involves blanching and drying the kale leaves. This step is necessary in order to avoid a soggy tart.

1) Wash the kale, and then cut out the tough central stems that run the length of the leaves. (If you wish, you can save the stems for stock.) Roughly chop the tender green parts. Drop the chopped leaves into the pot of boiling water, and let them cook until they wilt – about 2 minutes. Drain in a colander. Run cold water over the leaves just to cool them. Then dump the greens onto the clean kitchen towel, and twist it to squeeze out as much moisture as you can. (Twist the towel over a bowl, and you can then drink the healthy green liquid, or save it for soup.) Finely chop the leaves.

2) Heat the oil and butter in a large skillet set over a low flame. Add the onion, cover the skillet, and let cook until tender — 5-10 minutes. Add the finely chopped kale, the cubes of ham, the salt, pepper, and nutmeg. Turn up the heat, and sauté until the kale is hot and the ham has slightly colored — about 3 minutes.

Add the vermouth, and let it boil until it evaporates — about 1 minute. Remove the skillet from the heat.

Before proceeding, center the oven rack, and preheat the oven to 400°F.

3) On a lightly floured board, roll the pâte brisée into a 12-inch diameter circle. Transfer the pastry to the rimless baking sheet, and let it chill in the fridge for 15 minutes, or in the freezer for 2 minutes.

4) Scoop the cheese base onto the center of the pastry, and spread it out, leaving a 2-inch border all around. Top the cheese with the ham mixture, and sprinkle on a handful of shredded Swiss cheese. Fold the border over the filling, making pleats every two inches or so.

5) Bake in the preheated 400° oven until the cheese melts and the pastry browns — 35-40 minutes. Immediately slide the tart onto a wire rack, and let it cool for at least 5 minutes. Then transfer the tart to a wooden board for easy slicing.

Serve warm or at room temperature.

Mushroom, Spinach & Rosemary Tart

The first time I made this tart, I ate the whole thing all by my lonesome. Yes, it's *that* delicious. I'd advise sharing it with company at a casual spring or summer dinner party along with a large green salad.

Wine suggestion: Côtes du Rhône Blanc

Ingredients for
4 servings

For the filling:

1 tablespoon unsalted butter

1 tablespoon olive oil

1 medium yellow
onion, minced

4 cups sliced mushrooms

1 box frozen spinach
(10-ounces), thawed, drained,
squeezed dry in a towel, and
finely chopped*

1/2 tablespoon minced fresh
rosemary leaves

1/2 teaspoon salt and freshly
ground black pepper, or
to taste

1/4 cup dry vermouth

For the crust:

Pâte Brisée (page 124)

For the cheese base:

1 cup ricotta cheese blended
with 1/2 cup finely-shredded
Asiago cheese and 1/2
tablespoon minced fresh
rosemary leaves

For topping the tart:

A sprinkling of finely shredded
Asiago cheese

*You can substitute 1 1/2-2
pounds fresh spinach for the
frozen. Blanch and squeeze
dry in a towel as described for
the kale in the previous recipe.

Special Equipment:
A rimless, 15 x 14-inch (or
larger) baking sheet (or
use a rimmed baking sheet
turned upside down), lightly
buttered or sprayed with
vegetable spray

1) In a large skillet, heat the butter and oil over a medium-high flame. After the butter melts and the foam subsides, stir in the onion, mushrooms, spinach, and rosemary. Season with salt and pepper. Cover the skillet, lower the heat, and cook until the onions and mushrooms are soft – about 5 minutes. Then uncover the skillet, raise the heat slightly, and stir the ingredients until the mushrooms render their juices – about 5 minutes. Stir in the vermouth. When the vermouth has boiled away, remove the pan from the heat.

Before proceeding, adjust the oven rack to the lower-middle position, and preheat the oven to 400°F.

2) On a lightly floured board, roll the pâte brisée into a 12-inch diameter circle. Transfer the pastry to the rimless baking sheet, and let it chill in the fridge for 15 minutes, or in the freezer for 2 minutes.

3) Spread the cheese base on the cold dough, leaving a 2-inch border all around. Spoon the mushroom mixture on top of the cheese. Then fold the 2-inch border of dough over the filling, making pleats every 2 inches or so. Gently pinch the pleats to seal.

4) Bake in the preheated 400° oven until the pastry browns — 25-30 minutes. Let cool for 5 minutes, and then slide the tart onto a wooden board. Dust with finely shredded Asiago cheese.

Serve hot, warm, or at room temperature.

Caramelized Onion and Blue Cheese Tart

This rustic tart was inspired by a similar one I tasted at Talbott and Arden in Hudson, New York. The flavor combination of sweetly caramelized onions and pageant blue cheese is nothing shy of spectacular. As with the preceding tarts, a green salad and a bottle of wine are the only accompaniments it requires.

Wine suggestion: Pinot Noir

Ingredients for 4 servings

For the filling:

3 large onions, peeled and thinly sliced (use the slicing disk of a food processor)

1 generous tablespoon olive oil

1 generous tablespoon unsalted butter

1 tablespoon sugar

3/4 teaspoon dried thyme leaves

5 ounces blue cheese, crumbled

For the crust:

Pâte Brisée (see page 124)

1 egg, beaten

Special Equipment: A food processor for slicing the onions very thinly; a Dutch oven for cooking the onions; a rimless, 15 x 14-inch (or larger) baking sheet (or use a rimmed baking sheet turned upside down), lightly buttered or sprayed with vegetable spray

1) Over low heat, warm the butter and oil in the Dutch oven. When the butter melts, add the sliced onions, and toss them about to coat. Then cover the pot, and let the onions sweat until soft – about 15 minutes. Uncover the pot, raise the heat to "medium," and stir in the sugar and thyme. Cook, uncovered, and while stirring from time to time, until the onions color to walnut-brown – about 20 minutes. Remove the pot from the heat, and let the onions cool to room temperature.

2) Center the oven rack, and preheat the oven to 400°F. On a lightly floured surface, roll the Pâte Brisée into a 12-inch-diameter circle. Transfer the dough to the rimless baking sheet, and let chill in the fridge for 15 minutes, or in the freezer for 2 minutes.

3) Spread the cooled onions onto the pastry, leaving a 1-inch border all around. Top the onions with the crumbled blue cheese. Then fold the border over the filling, making pleats every 2 inches or so. Pinch the pleats slightly to seal, and then lightly brush the border with the beaten egg.

4) Bake in the preheated oven until the pastry colors, and the cheese bubbles and browns slightly – about 30 minutes. Let the tart cool on a wire rack for 5 minutes, then slide it into a wooden board for easy slicing. Serve warm or at room temperature.

Purple Poulet
(Chicken in Red Wine)

The first time I made this dish, my spouse thought we were eating beef. Indeed, the wine had turned the chicken a pretty shade of purple, and the meat was so incredibly moist and tender that it tasted, even to me, like long-simmered pot roast. Serve the stew over egg noodles, Creamy Mashed Potatoes (page 120) or toasted bread.

Wine suggestion: Cabernet Sauvignon

Ingredients for 8 servings

3 pounds boneless, skinless chicken breasts

2 tablespoons olive oil

2 tablespoons butter

1 bottle (750 ML) good-quality Cabernet Sauvignon

12 ounces button mushrooms, quartered

18 small "boiling" onions, blanched and peeled*

5 cloves garlic, peeled and minced

2 Turkish bay leaves

1/2 teaspoon dried thyme leaves (triple the amount for fresh, chopped leaves)

1/2 teaspoon salt, and grinds of black pepper to taste

2 1/2 tablespoons cornstarch blended with 1/3 cup cold water

*To make the onions easy to peel, first blanch them for 30 seconds in boiling water. Then use a small, sharp knife to cut off the root end and remove the papery skin.

Special Equipment: a skillet for browning the chicken and mushrooms; a 5-quart Dutch oven; a colander; a saucepan that will hold at least 2 quarts of liquid

1) Roughly cut the chicken breasts into 1-inch morsels. Blot the morsels dry with paper towels (wet chicken won't brown properly). Set the skillet over medium heat, and add 1 tablespoon of oil and the same amount of butter. When the butter melts and the foam subsides, add the chicken in batches, and sauté until brown – about 3 minutes. Transfer the chicken to the Dutch oven.

2) Pour 1 cup of wine into the skillet, and let it come to a boil while you scrape up, with a wooden spoon or spatula, the stuck-on bits of chicken. Pour this deglazing sauce over the chicken.

3) Add the remaining oil and butter to the skillet. When the butter stops foaming, add the quartered mushrooms and sauté until they begin to color – about 4 minutes. Tip the mushrooms into the Dutch oven.

4) Adjust the oven rack to the lower-middle position, and preheat the oven to oven to 325°F. Add the onions, garlic, baby leaves, thyme, salt, pepper, and the remaining wine to the Dutch oven. If the wine doesn't cover the ingredients, make up the difference with water. Bring to a simmer on the stovetop, then put on the lid, and transfer to the preheated oven. Cook for exactly 30 minutes.

5) Set the colander over a large bowl. Pour the stew into the colander, remove the bay leaves, and let all the wine-y liquid – you should have 2 1/2 – 3 cups — drip into the bowl. Return the contents of the colander to the Dutch oven.

6) Pour the liquid (you should have 2 1/2 – 3 cups) into a 2-quart saucepan set over high heat. Add the cornstarch mixture and whisk constantly until a boil is reached. Pour the sauce into the casserole, and stir gently to insure every ingredient is sumptuously coated. Taste carefully for seasonings – you might like to add more salt.

Purple Poulet is best when eaten the same day it is made.

Chicken with 40 Cloves of Garlic in 30 Minutes

My version of this dish is super-easy to make, yet it successfully replicates the French bistro classic. The garlic, which mercifully doesn't require peeling, becomes soft and sweet as it cooks. Your guests will enjoy popping a clove out of its skin, and spreading it on a piece of chicken or a crusty hunk of baguette. In addition, serve with a side of steamed broccoli or blanched green beans.

Wine suggestion: Pinot Grigio

Ingredients for 4 servings

4 heads of garlic, the cloves separated but not peeled

3 tablespoons unsalted butter

2 tablespoons olive oil

8 skinless, boneless chicken thighs

Salt and freshly ground pepper, to taste

1/2 teaspoon dried thyme leaves

1/4 cup dry French vermouth

Special Equipment:
a heavy skillet with a lid;
a medium saucepan

1) In the saucepan, bring 2 cups of water to a boil over high heat. Add the garlic, lower the heat, and let simmer quietly for 10 minutes. Meanwhile, put the oil and 2 tablespoons of butter in the skillet. Heat over a medium flame until the butter melts, and the foam subsides. Lay the chicken thighs in the hot fat, and brown them on both sides. Season with the salt, pepper, and thyme.

2) Using a slotted spoon, transfer the garlic to the skillet, placing the cloves on top of and in between the chicken pieces. Reduce the heat to "low," cover the skillet, and let the chicken simmer until done – about 20 minutes. Transfer the thighs and garlic to a serving platter.

3) Pour the vermouth into the skillet, increase the heat, and let the liquid boil and reduce slightly while you scrape up the stuck on bits of chicken and garlic with a wooden spatula. Off heat, add the final tablespoon of butter, and swirl it around until it melts. Pour the sauce over the chicken, and serve.

Chicken and Mushrooms in Tarragon Cream

Not to name-drop (okay, precisely to name-drop), but I served this for the main course when film director James Ivory (*Room with a View, Howard's End, Remains of the Day*, etc.) came to dinner. It's a simple sauté of chicken and mushrooms, enrobed in a cream sauce perfumed with tarragon. You can double or triple the recipe depending on the size of your guest list. Finish the meal by watching *Mr. and Mrs. Bridges* – another cinematic treasure from James Ivory.

Wine suggestion: California Red Zinfandel

Ingredients for 2-4 servings, depending on appetites

2 large skinless, boneless chicken breasts, sliced lengthwise in half to form 4 breasts

Kosher salt and freshly ground black pepper to taste

1/2 cup all-purpose flour (or a gluten-free substitute)

2 tablespoons unsalted butter, divided

1 tablespoon olive oil

3 cups sliced mushrooms

3 tablespoons finely chopped scallions (the white and tender green parts)

1/4 cup dry French vermouth

1/3 cup low- or no-salt chicken stock

1/3 cup heavy cream

1 tablespoon dried tarragon (triple the amount for fresh, chopped leaves)

Garnish: a handful of minced, fresh parsley

Special Equipment:
A large, heavy skillet

1) Pour the flour into a pie plate. Season both sides of the chicken with salt and pepper. Then lightly dredge the chicken in the flour.

2) Warm 1 tablespoon of butter and the olive oil in the skillet over medium heat. When the butter melts and its foam subsides, add the breasts, and cook them until brown and slightly springy to the touch – about 4 minutes per side. Transfer the chicken to a plate.

3) Melt the remaining butter in the skillet. Add the mushrooms and scallions and a sprinkling of salt and pepper. Sauté until the mushrooms brown — about 5 minutes. Add the vermouth and chicken stock, and let them simmer for 2 minutes. Then add the heavy cream and tarragon. Stir until the liquid begins to thicken — about 1 minute. Return the chicken to the pan and baste it several times with the sauce.

To serve, place the chicken on a warm platter, and spoon on the mushrooms and sauce. Garnish with the minced parsley.

Chicken with Herbes de Provence

Who needs the drive-thru when *real* fast food can be made right at home?
Fast to cook and inexpensive to buy are skin-on, bone-in chicken pieces. Sauté them
in butter and herbs, and in less than 30 minutes you'll have something crisp, juicy, and
succulent to put on the dinner table. Serve with a salad and, if you wish,
Hominy au Gratin (see the following recipe).

Ingredients for 3-4 servings

3 tablespoons unsalted butter

2 tablespoons olive oil or coconut oil

1/2 teaspoon kosher salt, and grinds of black pepper

1 teaspoon Herbes de Provence

6-8 skin-on, bone-in chicken pieces, or 1 cut-up broiler-fryer chicken

Optional for sauce: dry vermouth and heavy cream – 1/4 cup or slightly more of each

Garnish: Minced flat-leaf parsley

1) In a skillet that is large enough to hold the chicken pieces without crowding them, heat the butter and oil over medium-low heat (if using an electric skillet, adjust temperature to 250°F). When the butter melts, sprinkle the salt, pepper, and Herbes de Provence over the surface of the skillet. Add the chicken pieces skin-side down, cover the skillet, and let simmer quietly for 15 minutes. Then turn the pieces over, cover the skillet, and continue to cook until the chicken is done – about 5 minutes. The chicken is done when juices run clear.

2) Remove the chicken to a platter. If you are not serving with the cream sauce, simply tip the pan juices over the chicken, garnish with the minced parsley, and serve.

3) **To make the optional cream sauce:** Add the vermouth to the pan juices, and let it bubble while you scrape up, with a heat-proof spatula, the bits of chicken and and herbs which have stuck to the pan. Then add the splash of heavy cream, and let it boil and reduce until thick enough to coat a spoon – about 1 minute. Pour the sauce over the chicken, garnish with the minced parsley, and serve.

Variation: Chicken Thighs with Lemon

Take 6-8 skin-on, bone-in chicken thighs, and tuck a thin slice of lemon between skin and flesh. Sauté and season exactly as described for Chicken with Herbes de Provence.

Hominy au Gratin

Need a sexy side dish to accompany a Thanksgiving turkey, a simple hamburger, or the preceding Chicken with Herbes de Provence? Hominy au Gratin is your friend.

Ingredients for 8-10 servings

4 15-ounce cans white or yellow hominy (available in most supermarkets)

3 tablespoons unsalted butter

2 cups milk

1 tablespoon cornstarch blended with just enough water to make a thick paste

2 cups lightly pressed down sharp Cheddar cheese

1/4 teaspoon ground nutmeg

Salt and freshly-ground black pepper, to taste

Special Equipment:
a heavy 2 1/2-quart saucepan; a greased 9x12 baking dish

1) Center the oven rack, and preheat the oven to 425°F. Pour the hominy into a colander, and then run cold water over the kernels to remove the taste of the can. Put the butter and milk in the saucepan, and bring to a boil over medium heat. Quickly whisk in the cold cornstarch solution to thicken the milk. Off heat, add 1 cup of the cheese to the milk, and stir it around until it melts – about 30 seconds. Then stir in the nutmeg, salt, and pepper. Taste carefully for seasonings – you might like to add more salt and/or pepper.

2) Coat the bottom of the baking dish with a small amount of the cheese sauce. Then add the rinsed and drained hominy to the dish, and cover it with the remaining cheese sauce. Shake the dish a few times to help the sauce to settle. Top with the remaining cup of cheese.

Bake in the preheated oven until bubbly and browned – 30-40 minutes.

Variation: Hominy au Gratin with Ham. To turn this side dish into a main course, simply add 1 pound of cubed, smoked ham.

Irish Stew with Beer and Chocolate

Holy Shamrock, Batman! This is my favorite stew for St. Patrick's Day. The tender cubes of beef are subtly infused with dark beer, bittersweet chocolate, strong coffee, and local honey. For the dreamiest flavor, prepare and cook the stew a day ahead of time.

Ingredients for
8 servings:

5 strips bacon, diced

2 1/2 pounds chuck steak
(or "stewing beef") cut into
1-inch pieces

Kosher salt and freshly-ground
black pepper

2 large onions, roughly chopped

3 large carrots, peeled and cut
on the bias into 1-inch slices

3 parsnips, peeled and cut on
the bias into 1-inch slices

1 14.6-ounce can dark stout
beer (such as Murphy's
or Guinness)

1/3 cup strong brewed coffee

1 generous teaspoon
local honey

1/2 teaspoon dried
thyme leaves

1 ounce good-quality
bittersweet chocolate

2 1/2 cups beef broth

1 tablespoon cornstarch blended
with 2 tablespoons cold water

Herbed Mashed Potatoes
(page 120) for serving

Special Equipment:
A 5-quart pot or Dutch
oven with a lid

1) In a large skillet set over medium heat, sauté the bacon until it colors slightly and renders its fat. Transfer the bacon to the Dutch oven. Dry the beef with paper towels, season it with the salt and pepper, and then brown it on all sides in the skillet. Transfer the beef to the pot. Put the onions in the skillet, and sauté them until they soften – about 5 minutes. Add the onions to the pot. Tip the carrots and parsnips into the skillet, and sauté until they caramelize slightly – about 8 minutes. Into the pot they go. Pour the beer into the skillet, and let it boil while you scrape up, with a wooden or heat-proof spatula, the bits of meat and vegetables that have stuck to the pan. Add the beer to the pot, along with the coffee, honey, thyme, chocolate, and enough beef broth to cover the ingredients.

2) Bring the stew to a boil over high heat. Then lower the heat, cover the pot, and let simmer quietly until the beef is meltingly tender – 1 1/2 to 2 hours. Stir in the cornstarch solution to thicken the broth.

3) For each serving, put a mound of the herbed mashed potatoes on a plate, and make a basin in the center of the potatoes. Fill the opening with a ladle or two of the beef stew. This, my friends, is called "Delicious Living."

Duck Breasts Mirepoix

Contrary to popular belief, duck breasts are extremely easy to cook. I roast them on a bed of Mirepoix (diced aromatic vegetables) in a cast-iron pan, and they never fail to turn out precisely as they should: tender, juicy, and with crackling-crisp skin. This preparation is not only company-worthy, but cook-friendly, too. You can assemble the dish up to 8 hours ahead of time, and then pop it in the oven exactly 1 hour and 20 minutes before your guests arrive. Brown or wild rice is the ideal accompaniment.

Wine suggestion: Pinot Noir or Australian Cabernet

Ingredients for 4 servings (increase ingredients as desired)

4 large carrots, diced

1 medium yellow or red onion, diced

6 stalks celery, diced

Seasonings: kosher salt, freshly-ground black pepper, and dried thyme leaves

4 duck breasts

1 cup wild or brown rice, cooked according to package directions

Special Equipment: a well-seasoned 12-inch-diameter cast-iron skillet or a 9x13 baking dish

1) Put the diced vegetables in the skillet, toss them to mix, and dust them lightly with salt and pepper. Arrange the duck breasts skin-side-up on top of the vegetables. Season the skins with salt, pepper, and a generous dusting of dried thyme leaves.

Ahead of time note: Refrigerate the assembled dish for up to 8 hours.

2) When you are ready to cook, center the oven rack, and preheat the oven to 350°F. Roast, uncovered, until the breasts are fully cooked and their skins are crackling crisp – exactly 1 hour and 20 minutes.

Divide the breasts, vegetables, and rice between 4 plates, and enjoy while hot.

Root Veggie Pizza

I'm a great believer in eating locally (preferably out of my own garden), but that can be a challenge in winter months in the Northeast, when fresh vegetables are in short supply. Root vegetables are a mainstay, but how to make them exciting can be daunting. I came up with this novel approach to a "pizza blanco," or white pizza made with ricotta cheese. It turned out to be one of my favorite pizzas of all time.

Wine suggestion: Dolcetto di Dogliani Superiore

Ingredients for one 12-inch-diameter pizza, serving 4-8

1 medium 'Yukon Gold' potato (unpeeled), cut into 1/8-inch slices

1 medium turnip, cut into 1/8-inch slices

1 large carrot, peeled and cut into 1 1/2-inch-long matchsticks

2 medium parsnips, peeled and cut into 1/8-inch slices

1 small onion, chopped

Olive oil

Salt and freshly ground black pepper, to taste

1 thin, pre-baked, store-bought pizza crust

1 cup ricotta cheese

2 cloves of garlic, minced

1 generous teaspoon "Italian" seasoning

1 cup shredded Asiago cheese

Special Equipment:
A rimmed baking sheet (approximately 16x12-inches) for roasting the vegetables; a rimless baking sheet (or a pizza peel) for sliding the pizza into the oven. An offset spatula is useful for spreading the ricotta cheese

1) Center the oven rack, and preheat the oven to 450°F. Scatter all of the root veggies (except the garlic) on the baking sheet. Sprinkle them with the olive oil and the salt and pepper, and then toss them about with your hands until all are slick with oil. Put the baking sheet in the preheated oven, and give the veggies a toss every ten minutes until tender and beginning to caramelize – 30 to 40 minutes.

2) Put the pizza crust on the rimless baking sheet. Spoon the ricotta cheese onto the center of the crust, and then spread it out (I use an offset spatula here) to within 1 inch of the edge. Sprinkle the minced garlic over the cheese. Distribute the roasted veggies evenly over the crust, dust with the Italian seasoning, and top with the Asiago cheese.

3) Lower the oven temperature to 425°F. Slide the pizza directly onto the oven rack, and bake until the cheese melts and the edge of the crust begins to color – about 10 minutes. Slide the pizza back onto the rimless baking sheet, and then transfer to a wooden board. Slice and serve at once.

Poached Salmon with Crème Fraiche and Dill

The first time I made this main course, the Silver Fox proclaimed it "heaven on a plate." It's a symphony of salmon and vegetables, all poached together in a lemon-kissed broth, and served on a bed of baby kale leaves. It's healthy, low-carb, and devastatingly delicious. It's also one of the fastest dishes in my repertoire – just 20 minutes from start to finish.

Wine suggestion: Chilled Pinot Grigio, Sauvignon Blanc, or Sancerre

Ingredients for 4 servings (increase or decrease ingredients as necessary)

For the fish:

5 large carrots, peeled and sliced on the bias into 1-inch pieces

1 medium or large onion, peeled and quartered

1 lemon, thinly sliced

1 small sprig of lovage (or, substitute 3 stalks of chopped celery)

4 skinless, center-cut salmon fillets, approximately 6 ounces each, and about 1 inch thick

Kosher salt and freshly-ground black pepper

For th.e sauce:

6 ounces crème fraîche

2 tablespoons minced, fresh dill

2 teaspoons freshly-squeezed lemon juice

For serving:

Baby kale leaves – a handful for each serving

Optional: Boiled or steamed fingerling potatoes – about 3 per person

Special Equipment:

A 5-quart pot or Dutch oven with a lid; a flat, slotted spatula for lowering the fish into the water

1) In the pot or Dutch oven, bring 6 quarts of salted water to a rolling boil. Add the carrots, onion, lemon, and lovage (or celery). Lower the heat, cover the pot, let simmer quietly for exactly 10 minutes. Meanwhile, generously sprinkle the fish with kosher salt. With the help of a flat spatula, gently lower the fillets into the simmering water, on top of the vegetables. Water should barely cover the fish. Cover the pot, turn off the heat, and let the fish poach until it is perfectly opaque – just 5 minutes.

2) While the fish is poaching, make the sauce. Put the crème fraîche in a small bowl, add the dill and lemon juice, and whisk or stir to combine.

3) To serve, divide the baby kale and optional fingerling potatoes between plates. Put a poached salmon fillet on top of the greens, and dust the fillet with freshly-ground black pepper. Then, with the help of a slotted spoon, retrieve the veggies from the poaching liquid, and divide them between plates. Top the fillets with a dollop of the crème fraîche sauce, or simply pass the sauce, and let guests help themselves.

Shirred Eggs with Herbs & Garlic

When it's only me for lunch or supper, I find this French country dish is easy, quick, and absolutely satisfying. The eggs are broiled above a layer of heavy cream, and beneath a heady cloak of minced herbs and garlic.

Wine suggestion: Sauvignon Blanc, or a dry German Riesling

Ingredients for 1 serving

3 eggs

1 tablespoon fresh, minced parsley

1/2 teaspoon fresh, minced rosemary

1/2 teaspoon fresh, minced thyme

1 clove of garlic, minced

Salt and freshly-ground black pepper – a pinch of each

1 tablespoon finely shredded Parmesan, Asiago, or Romano cheese

1/2 tablespoon butter

2 or 3 tablespoons heavy cream

Toasted rounds of a baguette, for serving

Special Equipment: A small gratin dish (approximately 7 inches long, 5 inches wide, and 1 1/4 inches deep); a baking sheet

1) Adjust oven rack to uppermost level; preheat broiler on "high." Crack the eggs into a small bowl, taking care not to break the yolks. Mix the herbs, garlic, salt, pepper, and cheese together in a separate small bowl.

2) Set the gratin dish on a baking sheet. Put the butter and cream into the dish, and heat under the broiler until the butter melts and the cream starts to bubble – about 2 minutes. Carefully lower the eggs into the hot cream, and top with the herb mixture. Broil until the whites are set but the yolks are soft, and the cheese and cream are beginning to brown– 5-6 minutes.

Serve hot, and use the toasted baguette rounds to soak up the heavenly sauce!

Bucatini with Almond Butter Sauce

Bucatini is a fat, hollow, spaghetti-like pasta. For a quick lunch or dinner, I like to toss the strands with organic almond butter, rice vinegar, Tamari (a type of soy sauce), and sesame oil. Sesame seeds and freshly-snipped chives add the right amount of crunch, while red pepper flakes provide a whisper of heat. The dish is delicious at any temperature – hot, warm, or cold.

Wine suggestion: Gruner Veltliner

Ingredients for 2 large servings (recipe can be doubled or tripled as necessary)

1/2 pound Bucatini

2 tablespoons almond butter

2 tablespoons rice vinegar

3 tablespoons Tamari

1 tablespoon sesame oil

6 scallions, finely chopped

Toasted sesame seeds – about 1/4 teaspoon for each serving

Red pepper flakes – about 1/4 teaspoon per serving, or to taste

1) Boil the Bucatini in salted water until *al dente* (meaning tender, but not mushy). Drain the pasta, and then transfer it to a medium-size bowl.

2) Put the almond butter, rice vinegar, Tamari, and sesame oil in a small bowl. Blend with a wire whisk until smooth. Pour the sauce over the pasta, and gently toss with a spatula until each strand is coated with the almond mixture.

Divide the pasta between 2 soup plates, garnish with the sesame seeds and red pepper flakes, and enjoy.

Thyme and Wine Beef Stew

If a snowstorm rages and temperatures plunge to the single digits, my advice is to make a French beef stew. As it simmers, the stew will fill your entire house with the comforting aromas of thyme, red wine, garlic, and caramelized meat. If you wish, you can cook the stew on Saturday, refrigerate it overnight, and then reheat and serve it on Sunday. Yes – it's a stew that will wait for you!

Wine suggestion: Any dry, full-bodied red wine, such as Bordeaux, Claret, or Cabernet Sauvignon

Ingredients for 8 servings

1 1/2 – 2 pounds boneless chuck stewing beef

Olive oil

5 fat carrots, peeled and sliced on the bias

1 large white onion, chopped

8 large cloves of garlic, smashed and peeled

1 bunch flat-leaf parsley, roughly chopped

1/2 teaspoon kosher salt, or to taste

Freshly ground black pepper, to taste

1/2 teaspoon dried thyme (triple the amount for fresh, chopped leaves)

1 bottle full-bodied red wine, such as Bordeaux, Claret, or Cabernet Sauvignon

1 generous tablespoon cornstarch blended with enough water or wine to make a smooth paste

Special Equipment: A large skillet (or a big electric skillet heated to 350°F); a 5-quart pot or Dutch oven with a lid; a wire-mesh sieve

1) Dry the cubes of meat with paper towels (wet beef won't brown properly). Heat a glug of olive oil in the skillet, and, working in batches if necessary, brown the beef on all sides until a deep walnut-brown color develops – about 8 minutes. Transfer the meat to the pot of Dutch oven. Add a little more oil to the skillet, add the carrots and onion, and saute until the veggies start to brown and caramelize – about 8 minutes. Add the veggies to the pot.

2) Tip 1/3 cup wine into the hot skillet, and let it come to a boil while you scrape up, with a heat-proof spatula, the bits of meat and veggies that have stuck to the bottom of the skillet. Add this deglazing liquid to the pot. Also add to the pot the garlic, parsley, salt, pepper, thyme, and the remaining wine. The wine should barely cover the ingredients. Bring to a boil over high heat, then cover the pot, reduce the heat, and let simmer gently until the meat is absolutely tender – about 2 hours.

3) Ladle the stew and all of its liquid into a wire-mesh sieve set over a bowl. Transfer the contents of the sieve to a serving platter, and return the strained liquid to the cooking pot. Bring the liquid to a boil, then whisk in the cornstarch mixture. Whisk continuously until the sauce thickens – 30-60 seconds. Pour the sauce over the meat and vegetables.

Serve the stew over pasta, rice, or the mashed potatoes described on page 120.

Pea and Pinot Grigio Soup

This exotic-sounding brew was the result of poor planning on my part. I'd set about making pea soup one day, only to discover that I was 2 cups shy of the required 6 cups of chicken stock. What to do? Well, I made up the difference with Pinot Grigio. To my surprise, the wine brought out the earthy, "green" taste of the split peas. It complimented the smokiness of the ham hocks, too. I've never looked back.

Ingredients for 6 large servings as a main course

2 tablespoons olive oil

4 large carrots, peeled and sliced

1 large onion, peeled and minced

1 pound cubed ham (available in supermarkets)

4 cups unsalted chicken stock

2 cups Pinot Grigio wine

1 pound dried split peas

Seasonings: 1 teaspoon each kosher salt and dried thyme leaves, plus grinds of black pepper

2 smoked ham hocks (not "salt-cured") – about 1 pound total

Special Equipment:
A 5-quart pot or Dutch oven with a lid

1) Warm the olive oil in the pot or Dutch oven over medium heat. Add the carrots, onions, and the cubed ham, and let them cook, while stirring occasionally, until fragrant – about 5 minutes. Then stir in the chicken stock, wine, dried peas and seasonings. Bring the soup to a boil over high heat, then cover the pot, reduce the heat, and simmer slowly until the carrots are tender and your beagle's nose begins to twitch – about 90 minutes.

2) Remove and discard the ham hocks (or do your best to remove the scant amount of meat from the hocks, and add it to the soup). Gently stir the soup with a ladle to break up the peas. Ladle the soup into bowls, and serve with baguette croutons and goblets of (what else?) Pinot Grigio.

Linguine with Butternut Squash and Sage

What's infinitely-more interesting than tomato-based pasta sauce? Garlicky, herby, winter squash sauce! Toss it with sturdy strands of linguine, and you'll have a vegetarian main course that even meat eaters will love.

Ingredients for 6 servings

A 3-lb butternut squash, peeled, seeded, and roughly cut into 1-inch pieces

7 cloves of garlic, peeled

4 tablespoons olive oil

1 large onion, chopped

1 generous tablespoon fresh, chopped rosemary needles

1 generous tablespoon fresh, chopped sage leaves

1/2 teaspoon kosher salt (or more, to taste), and grinds of black pepper

2 cups vegetable broth

1 cup finely-grated Parmesan or Asiago cheese

1 lb. linguine, cooked al dente

Garnishings: For each serving, a sprinkling of fresh, chopped rosemary, thinly sliced sage leaves, and grated Parmesan or Asiago

Special Equipment:
An electric blender

1) Center the oven rack, and preheat the oven to 375³F. Put the squash and garlic on a baking sheet, and coat them with 2 tablespoons of the olive oil. Roast in the oven until perfectly tender and slightly caramelized – 50 minutes to 1 hour.

Ahead of time note: The squash and garlic can be roasted a day in advance. When cool, cover and refrigerate.

2) Meanwhile, in a medium-size skillet, warm the remaining olive oil over low heat. Add the onions, herbs, salt and pepper, and toss with a spatula to coat. Cover the skillet, and cook gently until the onions are tender and translucent – about 10 minutes. If the squash and garlic were prepared in advance and refrigerated, add them to the pan to warm them.

3) Tip the works into the jar of an electric blender, add the vegetable broth and cheese, and blend at high speed until a rich, thick sauce develops – about 30 seconds. If the sauce is too thick for your liking, thin it out with more vegetable broth.

Pour 3 cups of sauce over the cooked pasta, and blend gently with a spatula. Garnish individual servings with rosemary, sage, and freshly-grated Parmesan or Asiago.

Note: You'll end up with about 5 cups of sauce. Use 3 cups for the pasta, and freeze the rest. It will come in handy when you need a quick dinner for two!

Brown Rice, Lentil, and Kale Soup

Hearty, healthy, colorful, and fragrant, this soup warms all the right spots for me. And if you think it tastes great on day one, I have a pleasant surprise for you: it's even better on days two and three!

Ingredients for 10-12 servings

1/4 cup olive oil

1/2 lb. sweet Italian sausage meat

3 large carrots, peeled and diced

4 celery stalks, diced

1 large onion, diced

1 teaspoon cumin seeds

1/2 teaspoon dried thyme leaves

1/2 teaspoon kosher salt, and grinds of black pepper to taste

1/2 teaspoon crushed red pepper flakes

12 cups unsalted chicken stock

1/2 cup dry lentil beans

1/2 lb. kale leaves, roughly chopped

Special Equipment:
A 5-quart pot or Dutch oven with a lid

1) In the pot or Dutch oven, warm the olive oil over medium heat. Add the sausage, and break it up with a wooden spoon or spatula as it cooks. Sauté the meat until it browns – about 5 minutes. Use a slotted spoon to transfer the crumbled meat to a bowl.

2) Add the carrots, celery, and onion to the pot, and give them a quick stir just to coat. Then stir in the cumin, thyme, salt, pepper, and red pepper flakes. Cook, while stirring from time to time, until the vegetables start to color – about 15 minutes. Then stir in the chicken stock, sausage, rice, and lentils.

3) Bring to a boil over a high flame, then reduce the heat and partially cover the pot. Let simmer quietly until the rice is cooked – about 45 minutes. Then add the kale leaves, and stir them about until they wither – about 1 minute.

Serve hot, along with a hunk of crusty bread. Refrigerate leftover soup after it cools. Flavors will deepen after the soup has been chilled and reheated.

Portobello Mushroom Burgers

Portobellos are enormous, bronze-colored mushrooms. You can find them in almost any supermarket. Give them a garlicky marinade, grill them until tender, and you'll have a vegetarian "hamburger patty" that no carnivore can resist. Quinoa Stuffing with Leeks and Sun Dried Tomatoes (see the following recipe) makes a welcome accompaniment for the burgers.

Wine suggestion: chilled Pinot Grigio

Ingredients for 4 burgers:

4 Portobello mushrooms, their stems removed and discarded

1/4 cup balsamic vinegar

3 cloves of garlic, minced

1 tablespoon Worcestershire sauce

2 tablespoons olive oil (plus more for greasing the grill pan)

2 teaspoons Italian seasoning

Kosher salt and freshly-ground black pepper – a pinch of each

Toasted English muffins or hamburger rolls, for serving

Extras for garnish: Blue cheese dressing or ketchup; lettuce, tomato, and raw or sautéed onion

Special Equipment: a non-stick grill pan (or, use an outdoor grill)

1) Put the Portobello caps in a large, shallow dish. In a medium bowl, whisk together the vinegar, garlic, Worcestershire sauce, olive oil, Italian seasoning, and salt and pepper. Pour this mixture over the mushroom caps, and then flip the caps to coat the other side. Let marinate at room temperature for 15-30 minutes.

2) Brush the grill pan with olive oil, and then preheat it over medium heat. Set the caps curved-side-down on the hot pan, and cover with the marinade that remains in the dish. Cook for 5-8 minutes, depending on the size of the mushrooms. Then flip the caps, and flatten them with a flat spatula. Cook until tender – 5-8 minutes.

Serve between toasted English muffins or hamburger rolls, and garnish with blue cheese dressing, lettuce, tomato (if in season), and raw or sautéed onion.

Quinoa Stuffing with Leeks, Sage, and Sun Dried Tomatoes

I'm crazy about quinoa. It's a "super seed" with a delightful crunch and a neutral taste. Toss it with sautéed leeks, fresh sage, and sun dried tomatoes, and BAM – you'll have a gluten-free "stuffing" that won't leave you stuffed. Serve it as a side dish for the preceding Portobello Mushroom Burgers, or — if you are an omnivore like me – with roast turkey or chicken.

Ingredients for 10 servings as a side dish

2 cups quinoa

4 cups unsalted vegetable broth

2 teaspoons kosher salt, divided

2 tablespoons olive oil

2 tablespoons unsalted butter (or, substitute olive oil)

2 fat leeks, the white and tender green diced

7-10 fresh sage leaves, minced

1 teaspoon dried thyme leaves (triple the amount for fresh leaves)

Freshly-ground pepper, to taste

4 ounces sun dried tomatoes, finely chopped

4-5 cloves of garlic, minced

Garnish: 1/2 cup coarsely-chopped flat-leaf parsley

Special Equipment:
A 2 1/2-quart sauce pot with a lid; a large (12-inch diameter) skillet; a 9x12-inch (or slightly smaller) baking/serving dish

1) Tip the quinoa, vegetable broth, and 1 teaspoon of the salt into the sauce pot. Bring to a boil over high heat. Then lower the heat, cover the pot, and let simmer gently until all liquid is absorbed – about 15 minutes. Fluff the quinoa with a fork.

2) Warm the butter and olive in the skillet over medium heat. When the butter melts, add the leeks, sage, thyme, pepper, and the remaining salt. Sauté until the leeks soften and start to brown – about 8 minutes. Stir in the tomatoes and garlic, and let them cook for just 1 minute.

3) Pour the quinoa into a large bowl, add the contents of the skillet, and stir to combine. Transfer the mixture to the baking/serving dish, and keep warm in a 200°F oven until you are ready to serve. Garnish with the parsley just before serving.

Tabbouleh with Heirloom Cherry Tomatoes

When I crave something healthy for lunch, tabbouleh often seems the right answer. Do you know this vegan Lebanese salad? It's crunchy with cracked wheat, fragrant with parsley and mint, and bright with fresh lemon.

Officially, tabbouleh's only requirements are Bulger wheat (a/k/a "cracked wheat"), olive oil, the aforementioned herbs and lemon, plus a diced vegetable or two. For the vegetable component, consider diced zucchini, diced green beans, or diced anything-and-everything your garden or farmers' market can provide.

Ingredients for 2 servings as a main course, or 4 servings as a side dish

1 cup Bulger wheat

1 1/2 cups boiling water

The juice of 1 lemon

1/4 cup olive oil

1 teaspoon salt, divided

5-7 scallions, diced (use both the white and green parts)

1 young zucchini (not more than 8 inches in length), diced

Fresh, coarsely-chopped mint leaves – enough to equal 1 cup

Fresh, coarsely-chopped flat leaf parsley – enough to equal 1 cup

Grinds of black pepper, to taste

1 dozen (or more) heirloom cherry tomatoes, halved

For serving: Pita bread, cut into wedges

1) Pour the Bulger wheat into a large bowl. Stir in the boiling water, followed by the lemon juice, olive oil, and 1/2 teaspoon of the salt. Let sit at room temperature until the wheat absorbs the water and other ingredients – 1 hour.

2) Stir the scallions, zucchini, mint, parsley, pepper, and the remaining salt into the wheat mixture. Use a spatula to gently fold in the halved cherry tomatoes. Cover the salad with plastic wrap, and let it chill in the refrigerator for at least 1 hour. Taste to correct seasonings.

Serve cold with the wedges of Pita bread.

CHAPTER SIX

Delectable Desserts

Rhubarb Streusel Puffs

Three cheers for rhubarb. This perennial crop emerges in my garden the moment the snow has melted. I enjoy the plant's first tart stems on (store-bought) puff pastry dough that I sprinkle with crisp, buttery streusel. Hello, spring!

Ingredients for 4 pastries

4 slender stalks of rhubarb, cut into inch-long pieces

3 tablespoons flour

2 tablespoons granulated sugar

1/2 cup dark brown sugar

1 teaspoon cinnamon

A tiny pinch of nutmeg

3 tablespoons cold, unsalted butter, diced

1/3 cup "old fashioned" rolled oats

1 sheet store-bought puff pastry dough

Special Equipment:
A parchment-lined baking sheet

1) Center the oven rack, and preheat the oven to 400°F. Toss together the rhubarb, 1 tablespoon of the flour and all of the granulated sugar in a medium-size bowl. Put the remaining flour and the brown sugar, cinnamon, nutmeg, butter and oats in a separate medium-size bowl, and blend them, with a fork or a pastry-blending gadget, until crumbly.

2) Cut the puff pastry into 4 quarters, and transfer the quarters to the prepared baking sheet. Use a sharp knife to score a 1/2-inch border around each pastry square. Divide the rhubarb mixture among the pastries, staying inside the scored lines. Top with the streusel mixture.

3) Bake until puffed and golden – 20-25 minutes. Then transfer the pastries to a wire rack for 10 minutes or until serving time. The streusel topping will turn crispy as it cools. Serve warm or at room temperature, with or without a scoop of vanilla ice cream.

Blueberry Buckle

A buckle is named for its rustic or "buckled" appearance. It's a cinch to make, and it tastes like a poem. Just whisk up a pancake-like batter, dot it with berries, sprinkle it with sugar, and then bake it off. One hour later you'll have a puffed and golden dessert that you can serve at any temperature – hot, warm, or even cold. I like to top each serving with sweetened, softly whipped cream, or what the French call *crème Chantilly*.

Ingredients for about
6 servings

1 1/4 cups sugar, divided

1 cup self-rising flour

1 cup milk

1/2 cup (1 stick) unsalted
butter, melted

2 cups fresh blueberries

Special Equipment:
a well-buttered baking
dish, 9-10 inches in
diameter, and not more
than 1 inch deep

1) Center the oven rack, and preheat the oven to 350°F. Put 1 cup of the sugar in a medium bowl. Whisk in the flour, then the milk, and finally, the melted butter. Pour the batter into the prepared baking dish. Evenly distribute the berries over the batter, sprinkle them with the remaining sugar, and bake until puffed, golden, and fragrant – about 1 hour.

Blueberry Bars

If you are bored with the usual ubiquitous lemon bars, try my super-duper, perfect-for-a-picnic blueberry bars. These are deliciously moist, loaded with blueberries, and satisfyingly lemony. They will perk you up on a hot summer's day with a tall glass of iced tea or lemonade. You'll find these bars are delicious either cold or at room temperature.

Ingredients for approximately 24 1x2-inch bars

For the crust:

1 cup sugar

1 teaspoon baking powder

3 cups all-purpose flour

1/4 teaspoon kosher salt

Zest of one lemon, preferably organic

1 cup (1 stick) cold, unsalted butter, cut into a 1/2-inch dice

1 large egg, beaten

For the blueberry filling:

1/2 cup sugar

4 teaspoons cornstarch

Juice of 1 lemon

4 cups fresh blueberries, washed

Special Equipment: a well-greased (or vegetable oil-sprayed) 9x13-inch baking dish

1) Center the oven rack, and preheat the oven to 375°F. In a medium-size bowl, whisk together the sugar, baking powder, flour, salt, and lemon zest. Using a fork or a pastry-blender, cut the butter into the dry ingredients until the mixture resembles fine crumbs. Stir in the beaten egg. Pour half of the mixture into the baking dish, patting it down with your fingers until the entire bottom of the dish is covered.

2) For the berry filling, whisk together the sugar and cornstarch in a medium bowl. Then stir in the lemon juice. Add the blueberries, and gently toss with a rubber spatula until all are coated with the sugar mixture. Evenly distribute the filling over the bottom crust. Crumble the remaining crust mixture over the berries.

3) Bake until the top crust begins to color – about 45 minutes. Let cool on a wire rack for 30 minutes. Then cover with plastic wrap, and chill in the refrigerator for at least one hour. When ready to serve, cut the dessert into 1x2-inch rectangles. Serve cold or at room temperature.

Blueberry Galette

Sweet, juicy blueberries. Zippy lemon zest. Flaky French pastry dough, a/k/a Pâte Brisée Sucrée . Can you blame me for wanting to share this gorgeous galette with you?

Ingredients for 4 generous servings

For the crust:

One recipe Pâte Brisée Sucrée (page 124)

For the filling:

4 cups (2 pints) fresh blueberries

1/2 cup granulated sugar

2 1/2 tablespoons cornstarch

The grated zest of 1 lemon

2 tablespoons instant tapioca (to help absorb juices)

For glazing the crust:

1 egg, beaten

1 tablespoon Demerara sugar (or, substitute regular granulated sugar)

Special Equipment:
A food processor for making the pastry dough; a rimless, parchment-lined baking or cookie sheet

1) Make and chill the Pâte Brisée Sucrée dough as described on page 124. (The only difference between savory and sweet French pastry dough is the addition of 2 tablespoons of sugar.) On a lightly-floured surface, roll the dough into a 13-inch-diameter circle. Transfer the dough to the rimless, parchment-lined baking sheet, and let it chill in the fridge while you prepare the filling and preheat the oven.

2) Center the oven rack, and preheat the oven to 425°F. Put the blueberries in a medium-size bowl, add the granulated sugar, cornstarch, and lemon zest, and toss with a spatula to coat.

3) Sprinkle the dough with the tapioca, leaving a 1 1/2 inch boarder all around. Scoop the berry mixture onto the center of the dough, and then spread it out, with a spatula, to within 1 1/2 inches of the edge. Fold the edge over the filling, making pleats as you go. Brush the folded edge with the beaten egg, and then sprinkle the edge with the Demerara sugar.

4) Bake in the preheated oven until the crust is beautifully bronzed – about 25 minutes. Let cool on the baking sheet for at least 10 minutes. Serve warm or at room temperature, with or without whipped cream or vanilla ice cream.

Glazed Strawberry Tart

This tart is as delicious as it looks. The blind-baked crust is egg-enriched Pâte Brisée Sucrée, first spread with sweetened cream cheese, and then crowned with freshly-picked local strawberries. To make the berries glisten, I brush them with warmed red currant jelly.

Ingredients for one 9-inch tart, or 8 servings

For the egg-enriched Pâte Brisée Sucrée crust:

1 1/2 cups all purpose flour

1/2 cup confectioners' sugar

1/4 teaspoon salt

1/2 cup (1 stick) cold, unsalted butter, diced

1 egg, beaten

For the filling:

8 ounces cream cheese, softened to room temperature

1/2 cup confectioners' sugar

The grated zest of 1 lemon

40 fresh, medium-large strawberries, hulled

2 tablespoons red currant jelly (available in all supermarkets)

1 teaspoon granulated sugar

Special Equipment:

a food processor for making the crust; a pound of dried beans (or pie weights) for blind-baking the crust; a 9-inch-diameter removable-bottom tart pan; an offset spatula for spreading the cream cheese mixture; a pastry brush for glazing the berries

1) Pour the flour, confectioners' sugar, and salt into the bowl of the food processor, and process briefly to combine. Add the diced butter, and pulse 10 times or so just to break up the butter. With the machine running, pour the beaten egg through the feed tube, and process just until the dough masses on the blade – 15-20 seconds. Transfer the dough to a clean (not floured) work surface, gather it into a ball, and knead it briefly to insure that any stray flour is incorporated. Flatten the dough into a disk, wrap it in plastic, and refrigerate for 30-60 minutes.

2) On a lightly-floured surface, roll the dough into a 12-inch-diameter circle. Center the dough on the (ungreased) tart pan. Fold the overhanging dough inside the pan, and press it, with your thumbs, against the rim of the pan. This way, the sides of the tart will be thicker than the bottom. Prick the sides (not the bottom) all over with the tines of a fork. Place a big sheet of aluminum foil over the dough, pressing it into the contours of the pan. Then fill the shell with the beans (or weights), and freeze it for 30 minutes.

3) Center the oven rack, and preheat the oven to 425°F. Bake the weighted shell until set – 15-20 minutes. Transfer the shell to your work surface, and remove the weights and foil. Then return the shell to the oven, and continue baking until it colors slightly and feels dry to the touch – 10-15 minutes. Cool to room temperature on a wire rack.

4) Put the cream cheese, confectioners' sugar, and lemon zest in a medium bowl, and beat them with a spoon until perfectly smooth. Scoop the mixture onto the center of the baked tart shell, and spread it out evenly with an offset spatula. Arrange the strawberries in concentric circles on top of the cream cheese.

5) Mix the red currant jelly and granulated sugar together in a small, microwave-safe bowl. Microwave on "high" until the jelly melts and starts to bubble – about 45 seconds. Use a pastry brush to dab the jelly mixture all over the tops and sides of the berries. Refrigerate the tart until serving time.

Panna Cotta with Summer Berry Sauce

The first thing you need to know about this Tuscan dessert is that it is very easy to make. You can pour the mixture into individual custard cups, as I do, and then unmold these "cooked creams" onto dessert plates. When garnished with a sauce of local strawberries and raspberries, panna cotta makes a luxurious, silky-smooth finale that even the gluten-intolerant can enjoy.

Ingredients for 8 servings

For the panna cotta:

6 tablespoons cold water

2 packets (or 4 1/2 teaspoons) powdered gelatin

4 cups heavy cream

1/2 cup sugar

2 teaspoons pure vanilla extract

For the berry sauce:

1 cup fresh strawberries, hulled

1 cup fresh raspberries

3 tablespoons sugar

1 1/2 teaspoons freshly-squeezed lemon juice

Special Equipment:
8 (6- or 8-ounce) custard cups, lightly coated with non-stick vegetable spray

1) Arrange the prepared custard cups on a baking sheet. Put the water in a large bowl, sprinkle the gelatin on top, and let it stand, undisturbed, for 5 minutes. Meanwhile, tip the cream and sugar into the saucepan. Over medium-low heat, stir the mixture slowly and constantly just until the sugar dissolves – about 5 minutes.

2) Pour the warm cream into the bowl of gelatin, and stir the mixture with a spoon or spatula (a whisk will cause too much foaming) until the gelatin dissolves – about 1 minute. Divide the cream between the custard cups, and chill until set – at least 4 hours.

Note: When set, either unmold the panna cotta, or cover the cups with plastic wrap. Covered and refrigerated, the dessert will remain fresh and delicious for at least 2 days.

3) To unmold, first run a knife around the inside edge of the cups. Then set a dessert plate atop each cup, and invert the two.

4) Put half of the berries and all of the sugar and lemon juice in a small saucepan. While stirring from time to time, bring the mixture to a boil. Then reduce the heat, and let simmer until syrupy – about 5 minutes. Off heat, stir in the remaining berries. When cool or at room temperature, spoon the sweet sauce over the panna cottas.

Strawberry Soufflé

This is the show-stopping dessert I promise will end any dinner party on an unforgettable high note. Don't be surprised if your guests can't resist running their fingers around the empty soufflé dish to scrape up any remains. That's what happened last winter, when I served this airy pink confection to friends Robert Bluman, David Deutsch, Charlotte Sheedy, and Miranda Barry. Perhaps the copious amounts of champagne we all consumed helped lower everyone's inhibitions, but the soufflé was irresistible, I have to confess.

In the following step-by-step recipe, you'll find plenty of...steps. But fear not! Each step is easy to do, and if you follow them exactly, you'll have a dessert that rises to the sky, and tastes like a strawberry-scented cloud.

Ingredients for 6-8 servings

2 tablespoons softened unsalted butter, divided

1/4 cup granulated sugar

1 quart fresh or 1 1/2 pounds frozen strawberries*

5 egg whites from large eggs, at room temperature

1/2 teaspoon cream of tartar

1/4 teaspoon kosher salt

1 heaping tablespoon cornstarch

1 1/2 cups super-fine sugar

Optional for dusting: confectioners' sugar

Special Equipment: an 8 cup soufflé dish; a 30x12-inch sheet of aluminum foil; a food processor for puréeing the berries; an electric mixer for whipping the egg whites

1) Center the oven rack, and preheat the oven to 425°F. Generously grease the soufflé dish with 1 table-spoon of the butter. Add the granulated sugar, and swirl the dish to coat its bottom and sides. Fold the sheet of foil lengthwise in half, and generously grease one side with the remaining butter. Wrap the foil (buttered-side-in) around the outside of the dish and secure it with a paperclip or pin. The foil collar will insure the soufflé doesn't billow out of the dish as it rises in the oven.

2) Purée the strawberries in the food processor. Then transfer the purée to a small bowl or glass measure. Remember that you will need only 2 cups of purée for this recipe.

3) In a large bowl, beat the egg whites at low speed until foamy. Then increase the speed to "high," and beat in the cream of tartar, the salt, and the cornstarch. When the whites form soft peaks, gradually beat in the super-fine sugar (do not use granulated sugar, or your soufflé will have a gritty texture). Beating is complete when the whites hold their shape when scooped with a spoon.

4) Stir 1/4 cup of the whites into the strawberry purée. Then pour the purée over the whites, and fold them in with a spatula. (Fold gently to avoid deflating the whites.)

5) Set the dish in the preheated oven, and then immediately lower the heat to 375°F. Bake until the soufflé puffs, and the top forms a golden-brown crust – 45-50 minutes. Remove from the oven and unpin and remove the foil collar. Quickly dust the top of the soufflé with the (optional) confectioners' sugar, and serve at once, while it is still hot and dramatically puffed.

* I like to use frozen strawberries for this recipe. They are available at most supermarkets, and they are already washed and hulled. One and a half pounds of frozen berries (let these thaw overnight in the fridge) will produce the 2 cups of strawberry purée required for this recipe. Otherwise, feel free to make your purée from 1 quart of fresh, in-season strawberries.

The Best Lemon Tart in the World

Not only is this the world's best lemon tart, but it's also the world's easiest. For the filling all you do is put a sliced lemon (including the peel and pith) and a few other ingredients into a food processor and process for about half a minute. A slice of this year-round dessert is like a sunny holiday in Provence.

Ingredients for one
9-inch-diameter tart, or
enough for 8 servings

**For the egg-enriched Pâte
Brisée Sucrée crust:**

1 1/2 cups all purpose flour

1/2 cup
confectioners' sugar

1/4 teaspoon salt

1/2 cup (1 stick) cold,
unsalted butter, diced

1 egg, beaten

For the filling:

1 average size lemon (about
4 1/2 ounces), washed

1 1/2 cups granulated sugar

1/2 cup (1 stick) unsalted
butter, diced

4 large eggs plus 1 egg yolk

2 tablespoons cornstarch

1/4 teaspoon kosher salt

For dusting:

1/4 cup confectioners' sugar

Special Equipment:

a food processor for making
the pastry crust; a pound of
dried beans (or pie weights) for
blind-baking the crust; a 9-inch-
diameter removable-bottom tart
pan

1) Pour the flour, confectioners' sugar, and salt into the bowl of the food processor, and process briefly to combine. Add the diced butter, and pulse 10 times or so just to break up the butter. With the machine running, pour the beaten egg through the feed tube, and process just until the dough masses on the blade – 15-20 seconds. Transfer the dough to a clean (not floured) work surface, gather it into a ball, and knead it briefly to insure that any stray flour is incorporated. Flatten the dough into a disk, wrap it in plastic, and refrigerate for 30-60 minutes.

2) On a lightly-floured surface, roll the dough into a 12-inch-diameter circle. Center the dough on the (ungreased) tart pan. Fold the overhanging dough inside the pan, and press it, with your thumbs, against the rim of the pan. This way, the sides of the tart will be thicker than the bottom. Prick the sides (not the bottom) all over with the tines of a fork. Place a big sheet of aluminum foil over the dough, pressing it into the contours of the pan. Then fill the shell with the beans (or weights), and freeze it for 30 minutes.

3) Center the oven rack, and preheat the oven to 425°F. Bake the weighted shell until set – 15-20 minutes. Transfer the shell to your work surface, and remove the weights and foil. Then return the shell to the

oven, and continue baking until it colors slightly and feels dry to the touch – 10-15 minutes. Cool to room temperature on a wire rack.

4) Preheat the oven to 350°F. Cut the lemon into 1/4-inch slices, and remove the seeds with your fingers. Put the lemon slices, sugar, and butter in the work bowl of a food processor. Process until puréed – about 10 seconds. Add the whole eggs, the egg yolk, the cornstarch, and the salt, and process until a smooth purée is achieved – about 15 seconds. Put the tart shell on a baking sheet, fill it with the lemon purée, and bake until set – 35-45 minutes. The tart is done when the filling barely shivers when shaken. Let cool on a wire rack.

5) When completely cool, the tart can be covered and refrigerated for up to 2 days. When ready to serve, unmold the tart and dust the top with the confectioners' sugar.

My Very Serious Brownies

To my mind, these are the ultimate brownies. They are sinfully rich, super-chocolaty, slightly gooey, and not too sweet. You could serve them with pride to your book club. You could top them with a scoop of vanilla ice cream and a sprinkling of fresh raspberries for a company dessert. You could even use them to bribe your kids into cleaning their rooms. Or you can keep them all for yourself and refuse to share them with anyone. Not that *I* would ever do that . . .

Ingredients for approximately 24 1-inch-square brownies

1 1/4 cups (2 1/2 sticks) unsalted butter, softened to room temperature

1 1/3 cups superfine sugar

8 ounces good-quality (at least 60% cacao) bittersweet chocolate, divided

1/2 cup all purpose flour

1 teaspoon baking powder

Pinch of salt

1/2 cup baking cocoa

4 large eggs, beaten

Special equipment:
A standing mixer outfitted with the paddle attachment (or, use an electric handheld mixer); an 8x8-inch baking pan lined with parchment paper; a wire-mesh sieve for sifting the dry ingredients

1) Center the oven rack, and preheat the oven to 350°F. In the work bowl of the standing mixer (or in a medium bowl if you are using a hand-held electric mixer), cream together the butter and sugar until light and fluffy.

2) Break off 2 ounces of the bittersweet chocolate, coarsely chop them, and set aside. Melt the remaining chocolate in a heatproof bowl set oven a pan of simmering water or in a microwave oven that you monitor closely. While the chocolate is melting, sift together the flour, baking powder, salt, and cocoa.

3) Gradually beat the eggs into the butter and sugar mixture. Using a spatula, fold in the melted chocolate, then the chopped chocolate, and finally, the sifted dry ingredients. Pour the batter into the prepared baking dish, and smooth the top with a spatula.

4) Bake until the batter puffs slightly, and a wooden skewer inserted in the center comes out mostly clean (some crumbs will stick to the skewer) – about 40 minutes.

Cool completely before cutting into squares. Enjoy with a big glass of milk.

Rustic Apple Cake

Apple pie does nothing for me. I'd rather dive into a Rustic Apple Cake! It's the perfect finish for any autumn dinner party, and leftovers – if there are any – are delicious for breakfast or tea time.

Ingredients for one 8x8-inch cake, or 9 servings

For the topping:

3 yellow apples (i.e., 'Golden Delicious' or 'Crispin')

Juice of half a lemon

1 teaspoon cinnamon blended with 1/2 cup sugar

For the cake:

1 1/2 cups all purpose flour

2 teaspoons baking powder

1/4 teaspoon kosher salt

1/8 teaspoon ground nutmeg

1/2 cup (1 stick) unsalted butter, softened to room temperature

1 cup sugar

2 large eggs, beaten

1/3 cup neutral-tasting vegetable oil

1 1/2 teaspoons pure vanilla extract

Special Equipment: An 8- x 8-inch cake pan, greased and lined with parchment paper; a standing mixer (or, use handheld electric beaters)

1) Center the oven rack and preheat the oven to 375°F. Peel and core the apples. Then cut the apples lengthwise in half, and cut each half crosswise into 1/4-inch-thick slices. Put the slices in a large bowl, and toss them first with the lemon juice, and then with the cinnamon-sugar mixture.

2) In a medium bowl, whisk together the flour, baking powder, salt, and nutmeg. In the bowl of a standing mixer (or a large bowl, if you are using handheld electric beaters), beat the butter at medium speed for exactly 1 minute. Then add the sugar, and beat until the mixture is light and fluffy – about 3 minutes. With the mixer still running at medium speed, beat in the eggs, then the oil, and finally, the vanilla. At low speed, gradually beat in the dry ingredients, mixing only the flour disappears into the batter.

3) Scoop the batter into the prepared pan, and smooth it out with a spatula. Then arrange 3 rows of apple slices on top, fanning out each row so the individual slices overlap each other slightly. For best appearance, arrange the end rows in one direction, and the middle row in the opposite direction.

4) Put the pan on a baking sheet, and bake until the apples soften, and a toothpick inserted in several places in the batter comes out clean – 45-55 minutes. Cool on a wire rack for 15 minutes before unmolding.

To serve, unmold the cake onto a board, and cut it into 9 equal portions. Reserve the corner pieces for yourself, as these will have the crispiest crust!

Baked Apple Slices

Baked apple slices are noble things. They taste like apple pie, minus the crust. Spoon them over ice cream, oat meal, pancakes, and more. Just be sure to save some of the cinnamony slices for the Apples in Jack Daniels Custard (page 192).

Ingredients for 6-8 servings

3/4 teaspoon cinnamon

3/4 cup sugar

The grated zest of 1 lemon

8-10 apples (about 5 pounds), of a variety that will hold its shape during cooking (i.e., 'Golden Delicious')

The juice of half a lemon

6 tablespoons unsalted butter, melted

Special Equipment: A 9x13 (or slightly smaller) baking dish; a bulb baster

1) Center the oven rack, and preheat the oven to 375°F. Mix together the cinnamon and sugar in a large bowl. Then add the lemon zest, and rub it, with your perfectly-clean fingers, into the sugar mixture until fragrant. Peel, core, and quarter the apples; cut the quarters into thirds. Add the apples to the sugar mixture, and toss with a spatula to coat. Fold in the lemon juice, followed by the melted butter. Let the apples rest for 5 minutes while they exude their juices.

2) Tip the apples and their juices in the baking dish, and put the dish in the preheated oven. Every 10 minutes or so, tilt the pan and suck up the accumulated juices with the bulb baster. Redistribute the juices over the tops of apples. Baking is complete when the apples are fork-tender – 40-50 minutes. If the juices have not evaporated into a thick syrup, just suck them out with the bulb baster, and boil them down in a small saucepan. Pour the syrup over the apples.

Serve warm. Cover and refrigerate leftover slices for up to 4 days.

Apples in Jack Daniels Custard

I invented this delicious and unique dessert a few years back and have been serving it ever since. To make it, simply place already-baked apple slices in individual ramekins, top them with a Jack Daniels-infused custard sauce, and bake until puffed and golden. There's no better way to end a wintertime dinner party.

Ingredients for 4 servings

1/2 cup heavy cream

1/2 cup sugar

2 large eggs

4 tablespoons Jack Daniels whiskey

36 baked apple slices (see page 190)

Special Equipment:
Four 6-ounce, ovenproof ramekins

1) Center the oven rack, and preheat the oven to 400°F. (If your baked apple slices were previously refrigerated, warm them in the preheated oven until bubbling – about 10 minutes.) In a medium bowl, beat the eggs with a wire whisk. Then whisk in the cream, followed by the sugar, the eggs, and the whiskey.

2) Place 9 apple slices in each ramekin. Pour in the whiskey mixture, filling to just below the rim. Bang each ramekin down a few times to help the apples settle.

3) Bake until puffed, browned, and fragrant – 15-20 minutes.

Chocolate and Cabernet Sauvignon Cake

This isn't just a cake. It's the lover you've always wanted, and the ideal date for a Saturday night. It's dark, decadent, and delightfully delicious.

Ingredients for about
8 servings (or just 1 serving,
if you live alone)

2 cups all purpose flour

1/2 teaspoon salt

1 cup good-quality,
unsweetened cocoa powder (not
"Dutch processed")

1 1/4 teaspoons baking soda

1 cup (2 sticks) unsalted butter,
softened to room temperature

1 3/4 cups sugar

2 large eggs

1 teaspoon pure vanilla extract

1 1/4 cups good-quality Cabernet
Sauvignon wine

Confectioners' sugar for dusting

Special Equipment:
A standing mixer (or handheld
electric beaters); any standard
2-quart Bundt pan, including
the diamond-shaped
"Jubilee" model

1) Center the oven rack, and preheat the oven to 350°F. Butter and flour the cake pan (or easier, just spray it with "baking" spray).

2) In a large bowl, whisk together the flour, salt, cocoa, and baking soda. In the bowl of a standing mixer (or, use a large bowl and electric beaters), beat the butter and sugar at medium speed until light and fluffy – 3-5 minutes. Then beat in the eggs one at a time, followed by the vanilla extract. At low speed, add the dry ingredients and wine in alternating batches. Beat only until the flour and wine disappear into the mix.

3) Scoop the batter into the prepared pan, and lightly level the top with a spatula. Bake until a toothpick inserted into the cake comes out clean – about 45 minutes. Let cool in the pan for 5 minutes, and then unmold onto a plate, cake stand, or platter. When cooled to room temperature, dust with confectioners' sugar. Serve with unsweetened, softly-whipped cream.

Acknowledgements

First and foremost, thanks to the food and garden lovers who regularly visit my blog (www.agardenforthehouse.com). You are a daily source of inspiration. Without your constant prodding, I could never have completed this book.

Special thanks to Jennifer Josephy for editing the book's first draft. I appreciate your valiant attempt to correct my grammar!

To Charlotte Sheedy for insisting the Afternoon Tea chapter should remain in the book, and to David Deutsch for helping select the book's title.

To Sue Chiafullo, my beautiful, creative, bling-loving girlfriend. Thanks for the constant encouragement, and for reading, at the eleventh hour, the final 31,616-word draft of this cookbook. I owe you a drink. Or a car. Or a house.

To Brenda Johnson, my ever lovin' taste-tester. Thank you for intelligently evaluating my recipes, and for helping me to separate the wheat from the chaff.

To Gerald (Jerry) Miller, my best bud in Junior High School. I'm so glad you re-entered my life after a 30 year absence. Thank you for testing so many of these recipes in your Idaho kitchen. And special thanks to your mother, Juliette, who inspired my life-long love of French food. *Vive la buerre!*

To Tony Avenia, *sommelier extraordinaire.* Thank you for selecting the right wines to accompany the main courses in this book.

To Andy Milford for photographing me in the kitchen, and for videotaping my YouTube lifestyle series: *Kevin Lee Jacobs Delicious Living.*

To Lily the Beagle, an internet star as well as my constant companion in the kitchen. I could not ask for a better friend.

And finally, to Will Swift, a/k/a "The Silver Fox," the love of my life and my most ardent supporter. Thanks for waiting semi-patiently for dinner to be photographed before you could eat it!

Index